with love,
May

Rescued by a Gorilla

Mary Weeks Millard

Mary Weeks Millard

© Day One Publications 2016

First printed 2016

ISBN 978-1-84625-518-2

All Scripture quotations are from the New International Version 1984
Copyright © 1973, 1978, 1984

Published by Day One Publications
Ryelands Road, Leominster, HR6 8NZ

TEL 01568 613 740 FAX 01568 611 473

email—sales@dayone.co.uk

UK web site—www.dayone.co.uk

Cover design by ELK Design

Printed by TJ International

Dedication

For Jessica, may this book help you to love
God who loves you very much.

Acknowledgements

My thanks to those who took the time to read and commend this book.

My thanks to the staff of Littlemoor Library, who helped me research this book.

My thanks to Tirzah Jones and the staff of DayOne Publications, especially Mrs Chris Jones for her editing.

My special thanks to my husband Malcolm, for all his help and encouragement as I write these books.

Chapter One

It was September and the year was 1866. Every day the lord of the manor took a walk with his dog after lunch. He left his grand old mansion and walked down the long drive which was lined with beech trees. The leaves were now turning a beautiful golden colour and some had fallen, making a golden carpet on the grass. When he reached the large wrought iron gates, the gatekeeper came out of his tiny cottage and opened them for him, allowing the old man and his dog to cross the road and walk through the fields towards the Liverpool and Leeds canal.

These days Lord Mountjoy-Evans always took the same route and he stopped near the canal and leaned on his walking stick which had a silver top engraved with the family initials, E.M.E. As the old man looked down the canal towards Liverpool he smiled to himself, remembering the day in the summer when he had met a little girl who was working on this canal. The little girl, Winifred, had looked so like his own daughter, who had run away to get married to a farm hand many years before, and then, after talking to her she had showed him a handkerchief on which the same E.M.E. initials had been intertwined and embroidered.

It had been so amazing and so wonderful to discover that Winifred was his granddaughter and that she had a twin brother Wilfred, who was in a workhouse in a town a little further up towards Leeds.

He had been so sad to learn of the death of his daughter and all the troubles which had then afflicted the family that he decided he must help them. He had been able to help Wilfred, who he discovered had already left the workhouse and was working in a Dames' school, teaching small children and also studying with the teacher in the evening. When that school had finished for the summer holidays he had brought Wilfred to his home. Now, he had begun the new school term at a boarding school. Lord Mountjoy-Evans had sent Will to the same school which his other grandson, Ernest attended. He hoped that they would become friends.

Winnie had begged to continue her journey on the narrow boat which was taking coal to the Liverpool docks. She was working for a kind, older couple called Mabel and Dan. At first they had thought Winnie was a boy because she had run away from home dressed as her twin brother, looking for work. By the time they had discovered that she was a girl, she had already proved that she was strong enough to help them and they had become very fond of her. Indeed, Winnie had become like a granddaughter to them. Winnie had promised her Grandfather that on her return journey, once they had delivered the coal, she would leave the canal and come and live with him. That is why the old man came to the canal each day, always hoping that he might see the boat.

He loved watching the narrow boats and barges as they slowly made their way up and down the canal. Occasionally, he would call out to the workers on the barge and ask if they had seen the barge called, 'Bright Water' – hoping for good news.

The canal was an interesting place because in those days many goods were taken by water rather than by road to and from the large port of Liverpool. There was also wildlife like the little water voles that made their nests in the bank, occasional otters diving and the beautiful flashes of blue as the kingfishers darted around. Overhead he could hear the mewing sound which the buzzards made as they circled around looking for prey.

Lord Mountjoy-Evans whistled for his dog and began to walk back to his house.

"She won't come today," he thought to himself, "Maybe tomorrow. I know it will be soon!"

He thought about how happy his life had now become. He had been bitter and angry because his daughter had run away and he had refused to have anything more to do with her, but now he had asked God to forgive him for being so mean and unkind and had welcomed her children, 'the two Freds' as she had called them, into his life. He was already planning in his own mind to have a real family Christmas with all his grandchildren around him. How his dear wife would have loved that! She had died many, many years before, when his son, Ernest was ten and his daughter, Ernestina, only eight years old.

As the old man thought about his son Ernest, his smile disappeared. His son was an explorer and went all over the world hunting different varieties of butterflies and was working at present in the Congo, but it was now almost two months since there had been any news of the expedition.

He had letters most weeks from his daughter in law, Belinda, telling him about the adventures and activities of his three grandchildren who lived in Addiscombe, near Croydon. Ernest had now returned to Wheelie Hall School and entered the senior section. Elizabeth-Ann had a governess at home and their little sister, Elspeth was still looked after by a nursery maid.

Through the summer holidays the family had gone to Dorset for a holiday, staying near the parents of his daughter in law. It seemed they'd had all sorts of amazing adventures including chasing butterflies themselves! They appeared to have adventurous spirits just like their father!

Once back at his mansion Lord Mountjoy-Evans's footman helped the old man take off his walking boots and the butler came to ask him if he would like his tea in the drawing room.

"Yes please," answered the old man, "I think I would like the fire lit as there is a chill in the air and then I would like to toast some crumpets on the fire! I need some practice because soon, Winnie my granddaughter will come to live here and I'm sure she will like crumpets smothered in butter and cook's blackcurrant jam!" he said with a grin. The butler, Mason, smiled. It was so good to have his master cheerful again, instead of always grumpy and complaining!

"Violet has put a warming pan into Miss Winifred's bed, to keep it aired," he said. "The room is ready for whenever she returns. I'm sure she'll love having her mother's old room to live in!"

The two men laughed with happiness and while the tea was being prepared Lord Mountjoy-Evans went to his library and took the family Bible from the shelf. He had written the names of his two newly discovered grandchildren in it and the date of their mother's death and even the name of their father, Len Collins, inside the cover, along with the names of his son's family.

Len had been involved in a drunken brawl and sent to Australia as a convict for ten year's hard labour. The children had told their Grandfather that he had been kind and good until his wife became ill and then he had turned to drink, which had ruined their family life.

Chapter Two

Will was settling down at Wheelie Hall, his new school. It felt strange to wear the smart uniform every day and the collar of his shirt was stiff and starchy and he had red marks around his neck because it rubbed him. However, the tweed suit and waistcoat were warm and comfortable.

Will was in the junior school called the 'preparatory department, usually abbreviated to 'the prep'. The classrooms and dormitories were separate from the senior school, but on the same compound. Will had been to a local national board school in his home town, until he was put into the workhouse and had always been a good scholar and top of his class. In the workhouse he was so far ahead of most of the boys that the master had asked him to teach the younger boys and had also coached him himself, so that he could continue to do well. It had been that school teacher's encouragement and help which had got him out of the workhouse and a job as a teaching assistant at a school in a nearby town, which he had liked very much. It was there that his Grandfather had found him and taken him into his home and this term had sent him to boarding school.

Will had begun to learn Latin and Greek when he was working at the Dame's school, so wasn't too far behind the other boys in his class. However, most of them had come from well off homes and spoke beautiful English, whereas Will spoke with a broad Lancashire accent. Some of the boys at school had been bullying him about this and making his life a bit miserable.

Will had made a friend called Claude, who was also a new boy. Claude had lots of ginger hair which stood up on end and his face was covered in freckles. The boys in school soon christened him 'Ginger', which he didn't mind at all because it was the nick name given to him by his family. He was a cheerful boy with a smile for everyone and always seemed to be into some sort of mischief. He had three older brothers, all of whom were in the senior school.

"Take no notice of those boys," he said to Will, "They will soon get tired of bullying you and pick on someone else. Don't let them get to you!"

Will tried to take Ginger's advice, but he did feel a bit upset. He wondered what the boys would say if they knew that he had been in the workhouse and that his Pa was a convict. Probably they wouldn't speak to him at all and send him to Coventry! He hoped he could keep his past life a secret.

At the weekends the boys were allowed some recreational time. There were several games fields between the prep and senior schools and the boys from both parts of the school mingled together. It meant that families could meet up, so Ginger introduced Will to Joshua, Frank and Bertram, his older brothers. Like Ginger, they were all red-haired, had freckled faces and seemed full of fun.

"When we were in the prep we made a great den in the woods,"

Frank told them on the first Saturday afternoon of term. "Why don't we go and see if we can find it?"

All five boys were in agreement and went exploring at the back of the prep school. They climbed over the fence and ran into the woods at the back.

"Are we allowed here?" asked Will, not wanting to get into trouble so soon after starting at his new school.

"We used to go all the time and we never got into trouble," answered Joshua. "There is one place which I loved most of all. It is a little pond where the deer come to drink. You have to be quiet to see them – I don't suppose you'll see them because our Ginger doesn't know how to be quiet!"

The woods were quite thick, mostly beech, but some ash trees as well. The older boys led the way and took them down a narrow path. They had been walking some time when they came to an old stone wall, half buried by the moss and ivy which had grown over it.

"Great – it's still here!" exclaimed Frank. "This wall must once have been part of an old house. Feel carefully through the ivy and you will find a doorway.

"Found it," shouted Ginger, "Let's go in!" Will followed his friend into what must once have been a room, but now was just a space with three old, ivy covered walls and very overgrown with other bushes and weeds.

"It's just fab!" said Will, "What a great place for a den!"

"It doesn't look as if anyone has used it since we were in the prep," said Bertram, a grin spreading all over his face. "We used to have such fun here! We brought our tuck boxes and had Saturday feasts – and then would play cops and robbers in the woods. That's how we found the pond."

"If it's not breaking the rules, then I'd love to do that," Will answered.

The two younger boys looked at the three older ones and questioned, "Is the wood out of bounds?"

Joshua, the eldest answered. "There isn't a written rule, as far as I know. Most of the boys practice sport on Saturdays; some walk into town with Matron and others have visits from their families. We felt these woods were our secret place. Nobody else ever bothered to come out here."

"You see," continued Frank, who was the next eldest in the family, "We are all used to spending lots of time outside and exploring. Until we were sent to England to school we lived with our parents in Uganda. Father is a doctor and Mother a nurse and they are missionaries. That's why they don't come and visit us. We will see them when they next come home, but that will not be for another three years."

"I'm so sorry," said Will, "Where do you go for the holidays?"

"We visit different members of the family. Sometimes, we are with aunts and uncles and sometimes with our grandparents. Mostly it's fine – there is just one aunt who finds four boys rather a nuisance!"

Will was quiet for a few minutes. He realised that he wasn't the only one with an unusual family background.

"Most of the boys are alright, but there are some who give us a hard time because we are children of missionaries. They think our parents are weird because they work in such a remote country and want to teach the people there about God." Bertram told Will, "That's why we want to check that Ginger isn't being bullied. We have always tried to look out for each other. We have a baby sister at home and wonder how on earth she'll manage when she has to come to school or back to live in England. She's only two, so it will be a long time before that happens," he added.

"How about you, Will?" asked Joshua. Will had been dreading this question. He had kept as quiet as possible about his family background and even Ginger only knew that he lived with his Grandfather. He suddenly longed to tell these boys the truth. He instinctively felt that he could trust them and that they would keep his background a secret.

"If I tell you about myself and my family, please, please promise me that you will keep it secret," he begged.

The four brothers looked at each other, wondering whatever was coming. They were good and kind boys and they nodded to each other and all promised that Will's secrets would be safe with them.

"I come from a poor family," he began, "That's why I don't speak as nicely as you all do. I am trying so hard but I only know how to speak as a Lancashire lad. I am one of a twin. My sister, Winifred, is five minutes older than me. Our mother came from a titled family, but ran away to marry our father who was a farm labourer on their estate. They moved to a cottage in a small Lancashire town and mother had to work in a mill, even after we were born. When we were about six years old she became sick with consumption. Gradually, she became worse and worse. Through this time our Pa began to change. He started to drink a lot and hit our Mam and us. When she died it became even worse. He had no work and there was no money so he sent me into the workhouse and was sending Winnie to work in the public house, where Pa owed the Landlord a lot of money. The Landlord is a widower and he wanted Winnie as housekeeper to all his kids and it seems, he had designs on marrying her. She managed to run away, pretending she was a boy and working on the Leeds and Liverpool canal. Meanwhile, Pa got himself into a drunken brawl in which the Landlord was knifed. Nobody was sure what really happened, but since he had started the fight he was the one arrested and convicted. As far as I know, my Pa never owned or carried a knife.

He has been sent to Western Australia where they still take convicts. I heard his sentence was ten years' hard labour. At least he wasn't hung! He would have been if the Landlord had died. He wasn't a bad father, but changed when Mam became sick. I think deep down he really loved us all.

My sister, Winnie, managed to get a couple of letters to me, writing them in the secret code which we had used when we were small. On her way to Liverpool working the Leeds and Liverpool canal, she amazingly met our mother's father. I'll tell you that story another day! By this time I had been taken out of the workhouse and was a student teacher in a Dame's school in Skipton – and that story's also too long to tell now. Grandfather came and found me and said that he would take care of us from now on and he wanted me to come to this school and learn to be a gentleman. My cousin is also here, just moved up to the senior school. I haven't yet met him. His name is Ernest Mountjoy-Evans."

"Wow! That's quite a story!" said Bertram. "I know Mountjoy-Evans, he's in the upper third. I'll tell him that I've met you, if you like."

"I don't know what to do," explained Will, "I don't know if he knows my story and whether he will despise me."

"He's a decent chap," remarked Bertram, "Actually his Papa also works abroad, he's an explorer or something exciting like that. I won't say anything to him. Maybe he'll come and find you himself."

It was a great relief to Will to have told Ginger his background. He hated to be dishonest and he was so glad to have made a real friend.

"It might sound daft to you, Will," explained Joshua, "But this den also became our prayer place. We promised our parents that we would read our Bibles every day and pray for them. We tried to come here as often as we could when we were in the prep school. Maybe we can pray for your family, too?"

"Oh yes, please!" answered Will, "When I was at the Dame's school I had promised the minister of the church, who together with the workhouse school teacher had rescued me, that I would read the

Bible they gave me and also pray. I'm learning to love and trust in God, but find it hard."

So the boys sat on mossy stones and Joshua took a small Bible from his jacket pocket and began to read a few verses from the book of Jeremiah Chapter 29. Verse 11 seemed to stick in Will's mind, "For I know the plans that I have for you," says the Lord, "Plans to prosper you and not to harm you. Plans to give you a hope and a future." Then the boys prayed together.

"Now, show us where the pond is," begged Ginger. His older brothers laughed at him and they all followed Joshua down a path which wound through the woods even further away from the school. Suddenly, they came to a clearing and there in the middle was a pond – it was quite big and much to their delight, three deer were at the far edge drinking. As soon as they heard the rustle of the boys walking through the bracken, they darted away.

"I'm not sure that we will be able to find our way through the woods to the den and pond," said Ginger.

"We made notches on the tree trunks, so that we could always find our way back," answered Joshua, "Let's see if they are still visible."

The boys started to look carefully as they made their way back, first to the den and then to the prep school. Most of the marks were still there and Ginger and Will enjoyed hunting for them.

"We'll come next Saturday even if we don't get a chance to come any sooner," said Ginger.

"You bet–I think I'm going to like it at this school!" remarked Will.

Chapter Three

Most of the boys in the prep school had been there for several years, but Will and Ginger had joined the top class, the Lower Third. The other boys were not very welcoming to the new boys, so it was good that they had made friends with each other. In the dormitory the other boys played tricks on them – like making their beds into apple pie beds, so that when they tried to get in and go to sleep, they couldn't find the way in. The other boys were giggling as they tried to remake their beds. One night they found their pyjama trouser legs were sewn up so that they couldn't get into them! Fortunately, both Will and Ginger were good sports and joined in the fun and laughter and never told matron what was going on. Gradually, they gained the respect of their dorm mates – although they were still laughed at when they read their Bibles and prayed at the end of the day.

"Religious are we?" sneered the boy who seemed to be the form leader. "You'll get enough of that from chapel services every day and religious instruction from the school chaplain! You're not going to be much fun if you are religious maniacs! We'll soon knock that out of you!" he said unkindly.

Will felt himself going red, he was so angry. How dare these boys make fun of them! Then he tried to remember what Jesus had said about 'turning the other cheek' and not reacting badly. It was hard though – he wanted to punch them on the nose! Silently he gritted his teeth and in his head asked Jesus to help him not to fight. Suddenly, he remembered that it was his Pa's temper which had caused the fight and landed him up as a convict in Australia. The boys in the dorm seemed to want any excuse to have a boxing match and Will knew that he was no boxer. Ginger was less bothered. Maybe that was because he was the youngest of four boys. When the verbal abuse became too much, he sometimes got out his pea shooter and blew peas all around the dorm. He was a very good shot and several boys squealed as the peas hit their arms! Somehow, as always, Ginger could make everyone end up laughing!

The next Saturday came at last! Both Ginger and Will were longing to go and explore the den again. As soon as they were free they went to the tuck shop and took some treats from their tuck boxes. Will's Grandfather had made sure that he had a really good box, so much so that Will was able to share with Ginger, who had much less. His Grandfather had given him some money as well, but so far he hadn't needed to spend that at the tuck shop. He had bought some writing paper and stamps though, to write to his Grandfather and his sister, who he hoped had finished her work on the canal and would already be living in their new home.

It was a cool but sunny day and lots of the leaves had fallen from the trees in the wood, making it fun to scrunch them as they walked along. It also made it a bit easier to find the marks on the trees. They had no difficulty in finding their way to the den.

As soon as they arrived they found some mossy stones and sat down.

"Let's have a snack and then we can talk and pray," suggested Ginger.

Will produced some wonderful fruit cake which his Grandfather's cook had made. In no time at all every crumb was finished. Well, not quite every crumb, because a cheeky little robin crept very near them and picked up one or two which had dropped. The boys were thrilled to see it so near.

The sun had come out and it now felt quite warm – almost like summer. The boys talked about their week at school, laughing about the antics in the dorm, but Will was finding the other bullying hard to put up with. He was very shy when Ginger said maybe they should ask God to help them. He had never prayed out loud before and wasn't sure if he could find the right words. In church and in the school chapel everyone seemed to use set prayers with long words. However, when Ginger began to talk to God, it was just as if he was talking to his brothers or a friend, so when it was his turn Will copied him.

"I really need a bit of help, Jesus," he said, "One of these days I feel that I am going to get so angry that I will thump the boys who laugh at us. Please help me not to do that. I don't want to start a fight and I don't think I'd be much good at boxing."

"Maybe I could teach you a bit," said Ginger, "My brothers taught me in the summer holidays because they said I should know what to do before I came to school. Most school squabbles are sorted in the boxing ring – you need to be able to defend yourself sometimes."

"Oh would you? Thanks so much!" answered Will. Ginger got up and gave him his first lesson, about where to hit and how to dodge blows. After a while and another snack, the boys decided to try and find their way to the pond. They left the den and were finding their way down the path when Ginger almost stepped on a snake. It was sunning itself on a stone and Ginger was scared to bits. He hated snakes, for in Uganda as a child he had been warned many times about snakes which could kill with their bite or hissing their venom at him. He screamed at Will who was just behind him on the path.

"Run, get out of the way, there's a snake looking ready to strike!"

Will had no idea about snakes and jumped sideways off the path, screamed and disappeared from sight!

Ginger was now terrified. What had happened to Will? He went carefully to where Will had jumped and peered into a huge, dark hole.

"Will! Will!" he yelled, "Where are you? Are you alright?"

He heard a muffled sound. "I've fallen down a hole and stuck on a ledge. I think I may have broken my ankle, it hurts so much. It's very dark. Please help me".

"Stay still and hold on. I'll run back to school as fast as I can," yelled Ginger as he started off at a gallop. He ran almost nonstop back to the school and through the door calling 'help, help' at the top of his voice. Matron came running and two masters also appeared from the staff room where they were having a quiet cup of coffee.

"Whatever is the matter?" asked matron, looking at the terrified boy.

Ginger stopped a moment to get his breath and then told the grown- ups about Will falling into a hole. He was so upset and everything came out in a muddle. Matron and the teachers helped him to calm down and eventually they heard the story clearly.

"Get the groundsman and some ropes," suggested one of the masters, "and we'll need a stretcher and a blanket."

It seemed ages to Ginger, but in fact it was only a few minutes before he was leading them all into the wood and to the place where Will had dropped out of sight.

The place where Will had fallen was an old well. After a while Will's eyes became adjusted to the dark and he could make out a rusty old ladder going down the side of the wall. His fall had been broken when his foot had caught in a rung and he had landed on a sort of platform that jutted out from the side. A loose stone fell down the hole and after a long silence he heard a 'plop' sound. Then Will realised it was a well and the water was a long way down. It must be very deep. Will shivered. Had he not got caught in the rung and fallen on the ledge then he would surely have fallen to his death. He put his hand out to try and see if he could move back further onto the ledge. He was praying now, not worrying at all about proper words, but calling out to Jesus to save him from falling further and asking for Ginger to be able to get help.

When Will put out his hand, he touched something which seemed round and smooth. He peered into the darkness and to his utter horror, he saw a skull! The shock almost made him sick and for a moment he forgot the throbbing pain in his ankle. The skull was not big and Will realised that there were other bones close to it on the ledge. It must be a skeleton. Who had died down this well? Had another child fallen down as he had done and never been rescued? The thought made him cry out for help and pray again for Ginger to be quick. Thank goodness he wasn't on his own when he had fallen!

Will was trying to be brave, but the fright of the fall, the pain in his ankle, the terror of finding a skeleton and all the darkness around him were just too much. He found he was shaking with fear and terrified of shaking so much that he would fall off the ledge. He called out loud again to Jesus.

Suddenly, he heard in his head the words which Joshua had read the previous Saturday when they were in the den.

"For I know the plans I have for you," declares the Lord, "Plans to prosper you and not to harm you, plans to give you hope and a future."

It was as if Jesus had spoken directly to him. His terror went away and he knew that if God had plans not to harm him and to give him a future, then he would be safely rescued. Almost as soon as he realised that he heard Ginger's voice calling to him.

"We're here, Will. Hold on, help is here!"

It wasn't an easy rescue. The old iron ladder was so rusty that everyone was afraid that it might break, but with ropes they managed to haul Will to the top safely. The hurricane lanterns which they had brought with them revealed the gruesome truth of Will's discovery. There was a small skeleton on the ledge where he had fallen.

"Alright laddie," said the groundsman, "Take it easy. We'll carry you back to school on the stretcher, then I'm coming right back to board off this old well. Then I'll tell the police about the skeleton. That's their problem, not ours! Ours is to get you back safe and sound."

The rescue party helped Will onto the stretcher and the two masters carried it to the school. Once back, the doctor was sent for and Will was taken to the school sanatorium. Matron had to shoo lots of the upper third boys away as they crowded around wanting to hear the story of the adventure. Ginger was allowed to stay with Will until the doctor arrived. He examined the ankle and gave his verdict that it wasn't broken, just badly sprained. A few days later when Will was allowed back to school he found he was a hero. He didn't know why, for it had all been an accident. The most horrible part had been when he had discovered the skull – but as yet the police hadn't come up with any theory about it. Mind you, the Lower third had all sorts of ideas – so many lurid stories that the English teacher thought the best way to deal with the situation was to set a composition homework and get the boys to write them down!

Chapter Four

Libby-Ann was also having to do some writing for her English lesson. Life had been so boring ever since her big brother Ernest had returned to school at Wheelie Hall. It had been such fun during the summer holidays when they had gone to stay in Dorset. Libby-Ann so wished that she could go to school – even a day school would be better than having to do her lessons with a governess every day. Her little sister, Elspeth spent her time with the nursery nurse, while she did her lessons alone. It wasn't that Libby-Ann didn't like her governess, for in fact Miss Austerberry was kind and could be good fun. It wasn't that she didn't like her lessons, either, for apart from sewing which she loathed, she loved them all. She just wanted the fun of being with other girls her own age at school.

She had complained so much that day to her governess that she had been set the task of writing a letter to her brother. She sat at her desk in the day nursery chewing the end of her pencil and wondering what to write. Nothing exciting had happened since he had gone back.

"Dear Ernest," she wrote,

"Miss Austerberry said I should write to you today, but there is no news here. Mama has been looking very sad and sighing a lot. Since the letter which

came at the beginning of August there has been no news of Papa. Of course, Brownie and Cook keep telling her that 'no news is good news' but I don't think she believes it. I think she is worried because her forehead creases up with worry lines all the time and she doesn't go out so often to visit her friends.

I wish you were at home because I now have to have my dinner in the nursery with Elspeth. It was so much nicer to have it with you and Mama in the dining room.

Elspeth can count up to twenty now. I think she should have lessons with Miss Austerberry and I should be allowed to go to school. I shall ask Papa as soon as he gets home. I wonder what new butterflies he has discovered. We don't see any on our walks now because it is too cold and they have gone to sleep for the winter. (Libby-Ann wanted to put 'hibernated' but she couldn't spell the word).

Mama says that our cousin has started at your school. What is Wilfred like? She says that Grandfather hopes that we will all visit him at Christmas, so that we will meet the cousins. I do so hope Papa will be home by then.

Your affectionate sister (Miss Austerberry did have to help her spell this word!)

Elizabeth Ann Mountjoy-Evans.

It took her quite a long time to write this letter but once it was done her governess told her to put on her coat and hat and they would go for a walk and post it. Libby-Ann was pleased to hear that. It meant she wouldn't have to sew her sampler which she really hated doing. She loved to be outdoors and running around. "Why couldn't girls have as much fun as boys? It just wasn't fair!" she thought to herself as she buttoned up all the little buttons on her boots using a button hook. Girls had to wear hats and gloves and walk like little ladies. She wasn't at all sure about being a 'little lady'!

In fact, her governess had been thinking deeply about her charge. Earlier in the day she had talked to her mother because she knew that Libby-Ann was getting bored with her lessons and needed stimulation if she was to keep on learning. Her mother had readily agreed to a few changes, and one of them was that Libby-Ann might learn to cook. They both knew that cook wouldn't welcome Libby-Ann in her kitchen, so once they had posted the letter to Ernest, Miss Austerberry took her pupil up the Shirley Road and into the Combe Woods. Here they had a nature walk. Libby-Ann picked up as many coloured leaves as she could find and put them in a paper bag. She was going to press them and learn from which trees they had fallen. They had also taken Rex with them and he had a wonderful time chasing the birds and sniffing around the trees. At one he stopped and began to scratch and dig a hole. At first Libby-Ann thought he must have discovered a buried bone, but when she and her governess looked carefully, they saw that he had unearthed a dry, brown coloured lump of old fungus. Suddenly Miss Austerberry became very excited!

"Libby-Ann," she said, breathlessly, "I think this is a truffle! They are very sought after and expensive delicacies and the greengrocer would buy them from us for a lot of money!"

"Really?" questioned Libby-Ann. "It looks quite manky to me – why would anyone want that?"

"It's a secret ingredient that famous chefs use in the West End hotels – mostly truffles are imported from France. Let's hunt around and see if we can find any more. Rex, she added, patting the dog's head, "You are a wonder dog! Find us some more!"

Rex went away, sniffing around the trees. They didn't find any more truffles that day, but the ones they had dug up looked very good to Miss Austerberry, though Libby-Ann secretly thought that her lovely coloured leaves were much nicer!

"I talked to your Mama today, Libby-Ann," said her governess, "And told her that I thought you were ready to learn some new things. Nowadays girls are having lessons in many more subjects than they used to. I thought you might like to learn to cook, but we all know that Cook wouldn't want us near her kitchen, so your Mama said you could come to mine. My house is only about a quarter of a mile from here."

"That sounds fun," said Libby-Ann, skipping alongside her teacher. "I'm bored with sewing that horrid old sampler!"

"You'll have to finish it sometime, but maybe a break from it will be a good thing. 'A change is as good as a rest' as the proverb goes."

In no time at all they arrived at a little cottage on the edge of the woods. Even though it was autumn, there were still flowers in the front garden. Libby-Ann thought how sweet the cottage looked with lace curtains at the windows and a very shiny brass door knocker like a lion in the middle of the blue front door.

Miss Austerberry took a large key from her pocket and unlocked the door.

"In you go and take off your hat, coat and gloves while I tie Rex up in the back garden and give him a bowl of water. He must be thirsty after digging up the truffles!" she told Libby-Ann, who shyly entered the porch and entrance hall. The floor was made of tiles which had interesting patterns on them and gleamed in the autumn sunshine. She did as she was told and hung her coat and hat on the stand in the hall. In a few minutes Miss Austerberry joined her and took her through to the kitchen, where she stoked up the black range.

"Do you live in this sweet little house all on your own?" Libby-Ann asked her.

"No dear," replied her governess, "I have a niece called Alice, who is sixteen, who lives with me through the term time and attends a school in Croydon. She works very hard and wants to be a doctor. She tells me that a woman can have many opportunities these days and a lady called Elizabeth Garrett Anderson has trained to be a doctor and opened a hospital in London so that other women can train, too. Alice's ambition is to be a doctor."

"That sounds so exciting. I hope when Papa comes home he'll let me go to school. I would love to do something worthwhile like becoming a doctor." Libby-Ann replied, then added, "Of course, that doesn't mean that I don't like having you as my governess, but school would be such fun!"

"I do understand, dear. Maybe that will happen for you and I really hope so because you are a clever girl. I would miss you, but it's almost time for Elspeth to have proper lessons, so I would still have work to do," Miss Austerberry answered. "Now, how about a drink?

I think we are thirsty as well as Rex. Would you like some lemonade or would you like a cup of tea?"

Although the kettle was boiling on the top of the range, Libby-Ann instantly asked for lemonade. After washing her hands under the pump outside in the back garden, she had a drink of lemonade and a piece of shortbread.

"This is delicious!" remarked Libby-Ann, "It's the very nicest shortbread I have ever, ever tasted!"

"Then maybe that's what we should cook this afternoon and you can take some home to Mama," her governess suggested.

"Oh yes please," was the response of her delighted pupil.

"It's a good recipe for you to begin with because you only need three ingredients," said her teacher.

Come with me to the larder and we'll find them."

The larder was a very small room, not much bigger than a cupboard on the side of the kitchen but as far away from the range as possible. This meant that produce like butter and milk could be kept cool as in Victorian times there was no refrigeration. In this little old cottage there wasn't even gas lighting. Along the window sill was a line of candles ready to be lit when darkness fell and there was also a paraffin lantern.

Miss Austerberry carried a stone jar from the larder which contained flour (Plain flour).

Then she took a pat of butter which was on a plate and covered with a crocheted lace cloth to stop flies from sitting on it and some sugar which was in a blue paper bag.

They made sure that the wooden table in the kitchen was wiped clean. Libbby-Ann could see that her governess was as particular as Cook at home, who scrubbed her table every day. It was absolutely spotless! She went to a cupboard and brought out some scales, with a brass dish on one end and a box of brass weights to balance the other end. Then she found a big brown mixing bowl and a wooden rolling pin.

"Now you can help me with the weighing. First we need two ounces of sugar."

Libby –Ann carefully put a two ounces. weight on one end of the scale and then poured in some sugar from the bag, very slowly and carefully until the scale pan and the weight were exactly balanced.

"Good girl!" praised her teacher, as Libby-Ann poured the sugar into the brown mixing bowl.

"To make the sugar as fine as possible I squash it with a wooden spoon," explained her teacher. (These days we have fine sugar called castor sugar, but back then only regular granulated sugar was available).

"Now weigh the butter. We need four ounces of that. To stop the scale pan getting messy I like to put a square of greaseproof paper on it and put the butter on top."

Libby-Ann did as she was told. When the butter was in the bowl Miss Austerberry showed her how to beat the butter and sugar together with a wooden spoon until it looked pale and like cream. It took quite a lot of beating and her hand began to ache, so her governess took over and helped.

Once that was done, Libby-Ann could weigh the last ingredient, flour. She needed to have an '8oz weight' for that. At first she put too much flour in the pan and had to take a spoonful out to balance it. Miss Austerberry explained that she needed to be very accurate when measuring. If she made mistakes then the cooking would be spoilt. Once she had her eight ounces in the pan, her governess brought out a wire sieve and put over the mixing bowl.

"We need to sieve the flour before we use it," she explained.

"Why's that?" asked Libby-Ann.

"For two reasons. Firstly, to make sure the flour doesn't have grit in it or weevils and secondly, to allow some air into it. That makes the cooking better."

"What are weevils?" questioned Libby-Ann.

"Tiny insects which sometimes get into flour. You don't want to eat those!" was the answer.

Libby-Ann shook her head and sieved the flour *very* carefully indeed.

With the spoon she carefully mixed it with the butter and sugar until it all blended together and she could roll it out and cut it into fingers.

"Just one last thing before we bake it," she was told. "We need to prick it with a fork."

"It was fun doing that," remarked Libby-Ann.

The fingers were carefully placed on a flat baking tray which Miss Austerberry put into the oven part of the range. She had dropped a little water onto the oven floor and by this seemed to know that the temperature was about correct. It was a mystery to Libby-Ann but she guessed she would learn all about that in due course.

It baked slowly (275 -300 degrees f) for around an hour. While it was baking Libby –Ann had to write out the ingredients and method of making the shortbread in a new notebook which her governess had given her for her cookery lessons. She did this very nicely, because her teacher had told her that she might need this cookery book when she was grown up. There was one extra thing to add to the recipe and that was to sprinkle the shortbread fingers with a little sugar when they came out of the oven before they cooled.

Once all this was written down her governess took her out into the garden to play with Rex and also they picked some eating apples from one of the trees and put them into a basket.

Libby-Ann was thinking that they ought to be walking home because it was almost sunset and how would they manage the apples, shortbread, truffles and Rex when she heard a clip-clop and who should arrive but Brownie, their footman, driving the carriage.

"Your Mama arranged all this, so that we could have lots of time together to cook," explained Miss Austerberry – so we must put the shortbread into a bag, too. It should be cool by now."

"Can I taste one just to make sure it's as nice as yours?" asked Libby-Ann.

"Yes, of course. The cook should always taste her cooking. I guess Brownie would like one, too!" said her governess.

Brownie gave Libby-Ann many compliments on her lovely shortbread, "Don't tell her Miss Libby-Ann, but it's just as good as cook's, maybe even better!" That was praise indeed and Libby-Ann beamed, for Cook was Brownie's wife!

As they left the cottage Libby-Ann gave her governess a hug.

"It's been the best afternoon since the summer holidays," she said, "Thank you so much. I think I like cooking far more than sewing!"

When they arrived home Mama was waiting for her. She was so pleased to show her the shortbread and tell her about the truffles which Rex had found and give her the basket of apples which they had picked.

"Why don't you have dinner with me this evening," suggested her Mama, "Then you can tell me all about your afternoon."

"Can I really?" exclaimed Libby-Ann, "I so loved doing that when we were all together for the holidays, but when Ernest went back to school I thought you didn't want me on my own".

"Oh my dearest daughter," said her Mama, giving her a cuddle, "I've told you before that I love you so much, just as much as Ernest and Elspeth! Each of you is so very special and I think that maybe most nights we should have dinner together and you can tell me about your day."

"Can we pray for Papa, too and Aunt Tina's family and read the Bible together?" she asked, "It's hard to do that on my own."

"You are quite right, dear. I should have thought about it more. You must feel lonely up in the nursery once Elspeth has gone to bed. So long as I don't have to go out we'll have 'mother and daughter' time together every evening."

Libby-Ann was so happy. She couldn't remember being so happy for ages. Only one thing was still a problem. They hadn't heard any news of Papa for almost two months. It was very worrying. Was he lost in the jungle in the Congo?

Chapter Five

Liverpool was such a busy and exciting city! Winnie had never been to a large town and was just amazed when she, Mabel and Dan moored the barge full of coal, at the end of the Liverpool and Leeds canal. There was so much noise everywhere and so much busyness, after the quiet of the canal over the past few months. They had arrived safely a little ahead of schedule, which meant they would receive a bonus when they were paid for their work.

Dan and Mabel had become like grandparents to Winnie and were very protective of her when they arrived at the port. It was easy to get lost in such a big city and there were many pickpockets and thieves around. The old couple had made Winnie promise that she would not leave the barge on her own. They did take her out and show her around though. They walked along the docks where big sailing ships were moored. The sailors were chatting and friendly, calling out to people as they passed by.

"We're bound for the West Indies," called out a sailor as they walked passed. "We'll be back with a load of sugar! We are taking out passengers – want to join us? Plenty of room for a pretty girl like you!" he said to Winnie, who blushed with embarrassment.

"Nobody's goin' to hijack our lass!" Dan shouted back.

"That's why you mustn't go walking around on your own," explained Mabel, "anything could happen."

"Look at that ship!" exclaimed Winnie, "All the men seemed to be chained together."

"I think it is a convict ship," said Dan, "Probably going to Perth in Australia. Poor fellows, it must be horrible for them. When the ship gets underway they will be unchained and set to work. Last time we were here we were told that these trips were going to stop, but I did hear they still took convicts in Perth."

"I wonder if my Pa has reached Australia yet," Winnie said thoughtfully. "I hope he isn't treated badly. I wonder if I will ever see him again!"

"Now Dan, shut up!" said Mabel crossly, "Don't you go upsetting our lass. Did you forget her Pa had been sent out there for ten years?

"Sorry love," he said, patting Winnie on the head, "I had forgot. Sometimes I forget that you don't really belong to us and you are going to return to your Grandfather soon."

"That's alright Dan," answered Winnie, "You didn't upset me. I was just thinking about Pa. I pray for him every night that like the prodigal son in the Bible, he will one day say sorry to God and come into His family."

They walked further down the wharf and played a fun game of trying to guess what was stored in the warehouses which lined the docks, by sniffing!

"That one smells of spices," said Winnie, "Maybe they have come from India."

"I can smell coffee," remarked Dan and his wife said she could also smell tea.

Winnie had run away from home and found work with Dan and Mabel on their barge, 'Bright Water', by pretending to be a boy. When they discovered she was really a girl Mabel had found her some girls' clothes and now her hair had grown quite long again. She had saved all her wages and also her Grandfather had given her a gold sovereign to buy some new clothes in Liverpool. This was very exciting for her, but she had no idea where to shop and neither had Mabel. Mabel did know a barber who cut Dan's hair each time they went to the city. His shop was in a side street not far from where the barge was moored, so she took Winnie there along with her two beautiful plaits which she had cut off before she ran away from home.

Winnie was very surprised because the barber gave her several shillings for her plaits – he told her he could sell them to a wig maker he knew. Winnie's pile of money was even bigger, but where to spend it was a real problem.

Winnie and Mabel were staying in a boarding house for a few days while the coal was unloaded and all the business with the canal company was sorted out. Dan still slept on the barge looking after Clodhopper their faithful horse, who pulled it along and also making sure that no-one tried to steal their cargo. The woman who ran the boarding house was a very kind woman who knew Mabel well, so Mabel decided to ask her where they should shop, for Winnie needed smart clothes suitable for the granddaughter of a Lord.

"I'll do better than just tell you where to go," said the kind woman, "I'll take you myself. My niece is a saleswoman in one of the west end department stores. Our Sally will help you me ducks!" she promised.

So the next day they took a tram and went to the poshest part of the city. Winnie had never seen such lovely buildings before. They were tall and elegant and the department store seemed bigger than all the shops in Skipton put together! At first Winnie was scared. She looked round at the other shoppers and they were all elegantly dressed with hats, gloves and shawls. In fact she felt that people were looking at her and Mabel with disgust.

"Here's our Sally," said the boarding house landlady as she went boldly to a counter where a young woman was helping a young lady select some hosiery.

"Hello Aunt Ivy," the girl said, once she had taken the money from the young lady. "Fancy you being here. What can I do for you?"

"It's not me, it's for this lass here – she's the granddaughter of a Lord and needs kitting out!"

"Really," said Sally in surprise. "She don't look like one." Poor Winnie blushed at these words. She really did look like a street urchin, but she knew her life was soon to change.

Sally took Winnie and the two ladies to the children's section and they picked out some clothes – two lovely dresses, some petticoats, stockings, boots, a shawl, a hat, coat and gloves.

Then Mabel took her into a small room where she had to try

on all the new clothes. They transformed her. Winnie looked in the mirror and wondered who was looking back at her! Never had she had elegant clothes and they felt very strange.

"You look wonderful, love," said Mabel.

"But I don't feel like me anymore. I felt better in our Will's trousers and waistcoat!" she said.

"You'll soon get used to being a young lady. You will live in a big mansion with your Grandfather. Your mother would be so pleased!"

Thinking of her mother did make Winnie smile a bit. Maybe her Mam had looked like this when she was young. Her Grandfather had said she looked very much like her.

They took the clothes to the counter where the landlady had been telling Sally all about Winnie.

"It's like a fairy story!" she said, "Who would ever have thought it!"

"The clothes fit very well," said Mabel. Please can you tell us what the prices are? I think we have enough money. I've never bought fine things like these before!"

There was enough money and just a little over, so once the clothes were all tied up in a nice bundle, Winnie suggested that they all have a cup of tea together. They went to a nearby tea room and ordered tea and cakes. The waitress looked at them as if they had no right to be there, as did some of the other customers. Winnie sighed. She wondered if people would always stare at her as if she had no right to be the granddaughter of a Lord!

The tea was brought to them in pretty china cups with roses on them and a teapot and milk jug to match. The cakes were on a two tiered stand and looked really appetising. The waitress unfolded pretty napkins and put them on their laps and the landlady began to pour out the tea.

"This is good practice for you Winnie," she remarked, "I'm sure you will have afternoon tea with your Grandfather."

Winnie had thought it would be such a nice treat for Mabel and her friend, but now she felt miserable and out of place. Her hand was shaking as she tried to hold the beautiful cup in the way she saw the other customers did as they drank their tea. A boy who was about her own age sitting at a nearby table looked at her as if she were an insect on the floor. He got up and roughly bumped into her causing her to drop the cup of tea, which landed on the floor and smashed into pieces. Worse than that, her parcel of new clothes was soaked!

Poor Winnie was upset and shocked and frightened all at once. Mabel turned on the boy.

"Who do you think you are – behaving like that?" she shouted.

"And who does she think she is taking tea in an establishment like this? There should be a ban on folk like you coming to upper class places!" the boy said with a smirk.

Mabel had to restrain herself from hitting the boy, whose mother seemed to think the whole incident was a huge joke.

"This child is the granddaughter of Lord Mountjoy-Evans" said the landlady in a firm voice. "We all have the right to be here and our manners are certainly better than yours!" she said loud enough for everyone to hear.

Meanwhile, the waitress had come over to pick up the pieces of the broken cup and was about to scold Winnie for her carelessness when an old gentleman got up and walked over to the table.

""My dear child," he said, "I'm so sorry that you have been so badly treated and I am ashamed of the behaviour of this young man. Please young sir," he said, addressing the boy, "Leave these premises at once and I advise your mother to take you home and find a punishment suitable for your caddish behaviour. I own this tea room and from now on you are the one banned from coming here. Before you go I demand that you apologise to this young lady."

"Never!" said the boy and he ran out of the door with his mother following him, looking very red in the face. Once he had disappeared the tea room settled down.

"Please accept my sincere apologies that such a thing should happen on these premises," said the old man to the two women and Winnie. He asked the waitress to bring fresh tea and more cakes, all 'on the house' and sat them all at his own table.

"I must make amends for your parcel being soaked in tea," he told Winnie, who was struggling not to cry.

"They are my new clothes," she explained, "ready for me to go and live with my Grandfather. I fear they may be spoilt and they are the most beautiful clothes I have ever seen!"

"We shall have them cleaned for you and if anything has too much damage then I shall personally replace them. Allow me to take the parcel and arrange for the cleaning."

Winnie was afraid to let the parcel go. She had heard so much about thieves in Liverpool that she was afraid she might never see her clothes again, but Mabel smiled and agreed, so she gave them to the old man. Once they had all had their tea he called his carriage and asked them all to step inside it so that he could take them home.

They were driven to the boarding house in style and on the journey Winnie told the old man her story. He was quite moved to hear it and said that he could see she was a young lady of breeding.

"Never let anyone make you think you are not important or not good enough," he said. "It doesn't matter who we are by birth, it's what is inside that counts. Be truthful and courageous, kind to everybody no matter who they are. That is what matters my dear."

When the old gentleman left them he promised to return the following afternoon with the clothes for Winnie. This time she believed him and said 'thank you sir'.

True to his word the following afternoon he returned with the clothes as good as new. He also had a box of cakes for Winnie as well. She was overwhelmed at his kindness and was longing to take them to the barge and share them with Dan, who as yet had not heard of the adventure.

Two days later they were back on the canal. Winnie was glad to leave the big port of Liverpool behind and looked forward to the return journey and seeing her Grandfather again.

Chapter Six

Ernest was sitting in the common room for the upper third and lower fourth boys. So far he was enjoying being in the senior school, though he did have to 'fag' for one of the prefects. He was fortunate in that Joshua didn't boss him around in the way that many of the upper sixth prefects treated their 'fags'. Mostly, he only had to tidy Joshua's study and wash up his cocoa cup.

Two letters had arrived for Ernest and he was reading them before study hall where they did their evening homework. One letter was from his sister, Libby-Ann. He smiled as he read it. He could almost hear her speaking as he read the words. He was sorry that there was no news of their father – he thought that by now Papa should be on his way home again.

The other letter was from his Grandfather. Ernest read it with interest, for his Grandfather told him about the discovery of his two long lost cousins and how they were becoming his wards as their father was in Australia for a long time. His eyes nearly popped out of his head when he read that Wilfred was in the same school, but being two years' his junior was in the preparatory department.

"Please be kind to him," Ernest read, "His mother was your aunt and she has now died. He may need help as school life will be so different from everything he has known. I am hoping we will all meet up and celebrate Christmas together at Mountjoy Hall."

Ernest let the letter fall into his lap. His cousin was called Wilfred Collins. He had heard that name only last week. Joshua had told him about his youngest brother, Ginger, who was in the lower third and how they had all been out in the woods and Will Collins had fallen down an old well. Not only had he been hurt, but he had also found a skeleton. In fact it had given rise to lots of rumours throughout the whole school. Some people were telling ghost stories and others were making up murder mysteries. Nothing like that had happened in the school in living memory!

At first Ernest felt a pang of jealousy – not at Wilfred finding the skeleton, but because Ernest had always felt that he was Grandfather's favourite, being the boy who would one day inherit the Hall. The Mountjoy-Evans estate was wealthy and extensive and was entailed so that it passed down from father to eldest son. The girls couldn't inherit.

Then as quickly as he felt jealous, Ernest felt ashamed. He should be glad that his cousins had been found. His Papa's last letter had asked them all to pray for the family. Actually, with the new term and going into the senior school he had mostly forgotten to do so. Holding the letter in his hand he silently said sorry to the Lord for forgetting to pray and for feeling jealous.

The bell rang for study hall and Ernest folded the letters and put them in his trouser pocket and went to do his homework. He had a job to concentrate as he should. Afterwards he shared the news with his best friend Sam and later with Joshua, who had asked him to come and polish his shoes.

"Well, that is interesting," said Joshua, "He's my young brother's best friend and he's a really nice chap. He was quite badly hurt, so is in the school sanatorium. He would probably like a visit. It can be boring stuck in there."

When lessons finished the next day there was an hour free time before supper. Ernest took his letter and ran over to the prep school.

"Please can I visit my cousin?" he asked Matron, showing her the letter.

Will was on his own and was, indeed quite bored. His ankle hurt much less now and he wanted to be up and back in class, but had been told he would have to wait until the doctor visited again and gave his consent. At first he was shy talking to Ernest, aware that he didn't speak as nicely as his cousin and he also wondered how much he knew about his background.

"Your Papa is in Australia and mine is in the Congo," remarked Ernest – I wonder when we'll see them again?"

Will told him, "I think it will be ten years before Pa comes home. He's working, as far as we know, in a place called Perth in Western Australia. I'm not exactly sure what he's doing – he's always been a handyman getting work where he could."

"My Papa is an explorer and butterfly hunter," explained Ernest. "We hope he might be home by Christmas, but there has been no news at all since late July, which is very worrying. I want to be an explorer, too, when I'm grown up."

"I want to be a teacher," Will told his cousin, "I have been helped so much by a couple of teachers and I'd like to help children get on in life, too."

Then Ernest asked Will about his adventure in the well.

"I was really scared when I touched this round thing and found it was a skull," he told him. "The police are now investigating. There has been no report of any missing child. They say the skeleton is female and she was about seven years old. They think it may have been there for many years. The skeleton has been taken away for investigation and the well has been sealed off. I'm not sure if we can still go to our den. We haven't been told that the woods are out of bounds. There is a lovely pond there and we saw some deer drinking from it."

I 'fag' for Joshua, Ginger's oldest brother," explained Ernest, "he told me about what had happened."

"It's weird," said Will, "I was getting bullied because I come from a poor background and speak with a Lancashire accent, but now I seem to be some sort of hero and everyone wants to be my friend and hear the story! Ginger and I had prayed together in the den – we wanted it to be a special prayer space for us because we are both Christians but just beginners, so to speak. We prayed about the bullying, but it was a strange way to get an answer to prayer!"

Will was a bit shy about saying this to his new found cousin, but Ginger had said they must be bold and 'nail their colours to the mast' so to speak. He was surprised when Ernest told him about his father's last letter and how his aunt and cousins had begun to read the Bible to find out about Jesus and also to pray, especially for their aunt Ernestina's family.

"Maybe, I could join you and Ginger sometimes, for I confess I have not been doing these things since I returned to school."

So, that is how the cousins became firm friends. Once Will was allowed to be up and back to class as usual, he and Ginger began to go back to the den. Ernest joined them when he could and occasionally Sam came too. One Saturday Ernest came equipped with three quite large, horseshoe shaped magnets and some string.

"We've been learning about magnetic pull and things like that in science. I had an idea. If we tie long lengths of string onto the magnets we could go fishing in the pond with them," he suggested.

"Fishing!" laughed Ginger, "You can't catch fish with a magnet! You need a worm or maggot!"

"I didn't mean catch fish," explained Ernest. "You never know what has been thrown into a pond or lost by accident. Maybe we can find something of interest."

"I see," said Will, "It could be fun to have a go. So long as we don't fall in. I don't think Matron will let me get away with getting soaking wet again. We don't want the woods to be made out of bounds."

"We'll be careful," promised Ernest. "Last summer I found some treasure, but it looked just like an ordinary rock. It was called ambergris and a perfumer bought it for loads of money." As they walked down to the pond he told them the story of how he found the rock on a Dorset beach and how some young thugs had tried to steal it from him.

Down by the pond they made their magnet fishing lines. It was quite fun throwing the magnets into the water and dragging them along to try and attract anything metal. Ginger had the first find. He pulled up a rusty buckle. It wasn't much but he thought he would clean it up and keep it as a souvenir.

Ernest pulled up a nail, which really wasn't that interesting. He tried again, hoping for something better. Will then gave a shout.

"There's something on the end of my string, but it's too heavy for me to pull up. It begins to move and then drops off. Can you come and help. Maybe with three magnets we can lift it out."

Ginger and Ernest raced round the pond to where he was standing. They threw their magnets into the water near Will's piece of string. The stronger magnetic force began to shift the object. In their excitement Ginger almost fell into the pond. The other two grabbed him and pulled him back from the edge.

"Let's try to bring it up gently," said Ernest. It took four attempts before they managed to land a tin box safely on the edge of the pond. It was about twelve inches by six inches and was locked. In fact, it looked like a miniature treasure chest.

"How are we going to open it without a key?" asked Ginger.

The boys thought for a moment and then Ernest produced a penknife from his trouser pocket and tried to force the rusty lock open. It took a while, but eventually he did it. They opened the lid and gazed inside.

"Wow!" said Will, "This looks like another treasure! You must be an amazing treasure hunter!"

Ginger laid his pocket handkerchief on the ground and they emptied out the contents of the box.

There was a beautiful ring, which had tarnished in the box but looked like it was gold. It had a huge purple stone in it. Then there was a necklace, a smaller ring and a heap of old coins. They looked at the inscription on the coins and could just make out the king's head – it looked like Henry V111, but it wasn't possible to read the date.

"We had better take them back to school and show the head master," said Ernest. "You should do it, Will, because you are the one who found the box."

"No, we should go together," said Will, "Without your help I could never have brought it up and anyway, it was your great idea in the first place!"

"As you two are in the prep, I think we should take it there."

So the boys carefully put everything back in the tin, gave the magnets back to Ernest and began scrambling back through the woods. Will thought to himself that this had been a far nicer adventure than his first one. It still made him shiver to remember touching the skull and to think what might have happened to him had he not have fallen onto the ledge. Once again he said a silent thank you to God for saving his life.

Back at the school the boys burst into the entrance hall and ran to the head's office and knocked the door. He was not always there on a Saturday, but he had been catching up on office work and wasn't exactly pleased to see three boys burst in when he said, 'enter'.

However, after he heard the story and looked at the contents of the box, he was almost as excited as the boys.

"Well!" he said, "What a find! We must take it to the curator of the town museum and maybe the police. I'll go and show these things to Mr James (he was the history master) and get his advice.

I will keep you informed when I have news. You, Mountjoy-Evans, are in the senior school now, but I'll make sure you know when we have news."

"Thank you sir," Ernest replied, "Collins here is my cousin. We were doing an experiment together with magnets – it really worked!"

In the dorm that night all the boys gathered round Ginger and Will. They found it hard to believe that they had had another adventure!

"What is it about those woods?" asked one boy, "Why do you go down there anyway."

"My older brothers made a den there when they were in the prep and used it a bit like a chapel. They liked to go there and pray quietly and read their Bibles and we have decided to do the same," explained Ginger.

"I forgot, you lot are all religious nuts. Isn't your Papa some sort of preacher?" one boy said with a sneer on his face.

"Our parents are missionaries, that's why our home is in Uganda," said Ginger, with his usual cheerful grin. "I want to be a missionary, too. Maybe not a doctor like Papa, possibly a clergyman."

"So how about your Papa, Collins. Is he a missionary, too?" said another boy.

"No, but he does work abroad, in Perth, in Australia. That's why I live with Grandfather, Lord Mountjoy-Evans. My cousin Ernest was with us when we had this adventure. His Papa works in the Congo – also not a missionary, but a butterfly hunter."

The boys in the dorm took a while to think about this information and thankfully for Will, asked no more awkward questions. He didn't want to lie, but also wanted to keep some of his past a secret. The boys could be so mean.

"Why don't we have a midnight feast to celebrate our find?" suggested Ginger.

"Smashing idea," said another boy. All the dorm had taken food from their tuck boxes earlier in the day, so they pooled it all and after they were officially meant to be asleep, they lit candles and ate a fantastic feast. They had to be very quiet because if Matron heard them they would all be in detention!

Chapter Seven

During the next week the headmaster of the prep school asked for Ginger, Will and also Ernest to come to his office at the end of lessons. They were excited, hoping that he had news about the objects they had found in the pond. The museum was most interested and had cleaned up the coins. Their dates were all in the middle of the sixteenth century, around the time when King Henry VIII was on the throne. The large ring they thought might have been the ring of a bishop, the smaller ring was gold with a lovely ruby, but no-one knew anything more about it. However, the find had been so significant that the whole pond was to be dredged to see if there were any more treasures in it. The boys were to be invited to come along when that was done, since they had made the initial discovery.

Then the headmaster also said that the local newspaper would like to interview them about the skeleton in the well and the treasure they had found. The head said he would arrange a time for that and would be present to help them answer the questions. All three boys were excited and pleased they were to be included when the pond was dredged. Will wasn't so sure about the skeleton; it still gave him goose pimples to think about it.

They didn't have long to wait and were excused lessons the

following Friday afternoon when the history master escorted them to the pond. There were several men in waders and a couple of others in a small boat, who had a large net which they hoped to drag along the bottom of the pond. Some archaeologists were also examining the land around the pond. Already they had uncovered some low walls which were all covered in moss.

"Looking at old manuscripts and records, we think this might have been the site of a small Benedictine monastery and the pond was probably the monks' fish pond. The monastery was completely destroyed when King Henry VIII dissolved the monasteries. It is all very exciting!" they were told.

The pond gave up its secrets that day and many precious and interesting objects were recovered.

"I think the monks must have thrown them in the pond to keep them safe from the king's soldiers who wanted to ransack everything," their history teacher told them.

"I wonder if the well was also part of the monastery?" asked Ginger, "and even the ruins we use as a den".

"We will excavate the whole area, but maybe you could take us and show us where they are," asked the leading archaeologist.

The boys took him and he seemed to think that it was very likely part of the monastery buildings.

"I'm afraid that the woods will all be cordoned off while the area is excavated, so you will lose your den, they were told. The boys were sad about that, but understood.

At the end of the afternoon they had the interview with the newspaper reporter. He wanted the story from the boy's point of view. He said he would interview the museum curator and archaeologists later.

He told them something very interesting, too.

"In the paper's archives there is the story of a ten year old girl who went missing over a hundred years ago. It remained an unsolved mystery. We don't know the full story, but it seems you may have found her remains. Her name was Lucy Cooper and she lived about four miles away on a farm. She had gone out to collect blackberries but never returned."

"She could easily have fallen down the well as I did," commented Will, "It was covered by bracken, brambles and grass. If it was part of the old monastery then it may have been disused for hundreds of years and become overgrown. I hope it was that and nothing sinister happened to Lucy."

"When the coroner has examined the remains, we may know if it was an accident or foul play," the reporter told them. "Anyway, thank you for telling me your stories. I promise I'll tell you if I find out anything else. My editor will be very pleased. Nothing as exciting as this has happened in our area for decades. We should sell lots of papers!"

After he had left, the headmaster and the history teacher told the boys that the woods did in fact belong to the school. It would be out of bounds from now on but the whole school would be kept informed about all the developments.

"To think that we have an old monastery in our grounds and we had no idea!" said the headmaster in amazement. "I'm glad you lads went exploring and even fishing with magnets!"

When Ernest was 'fagging' for Joshua that evening he told him all about the exciting afternoon at the pond and then with the reporter and of course, Ginger and Will told all their dorm mates, so the story spread like wild fire throughout the whole school.

Meanwhile, Will's twin sister Winnie was working a huge flight of locks. Although a lock keeper helped, it was still such hard work that she wished Will was there to help her. She was still a bit scared of working the locks ever since she had fallen into one, very early on when she first began her time working on the canal. She had to manage with just a little help from Mabel, because Dan was needed to steer the boat safely through the locks. One bang against the lock wall and the boat could be badly damaged. It was like taking the boat up a steep water staircase. It amazed her to think of the navvies who had dug the flight and made the canal. How hard they must have had to work! Maybe her Pa was having to work like that in Australia.

In some ways Winnie was glad that she was going to live with her Grandfather, but in other ways she knew it would be very hard to leave Mabel and Dan. They had looked after her so well and she wondered how they would manage without someone young to help them. She knew that they would like to retire and live in the country, but the boat belonged to the Canal Company and so they had nowhere to live and very little money to rent a cottage. Even the old horse, Clodhopper, ought to be retired. Winnie worried about them all.

As she pushed back the lock gates and allowed the water to flow out she found herself praying.

"Please work things out for us all Lord Jesus," she said quietly, "You are our Good Shepherd, please look after us all."

Living with Dan and Mabel she had read the Bible to them every evening – the Bible her mother had given her before she died. Dan and Mabel had explained things to her and she had grown to love Jesus even as they did. She knew she would miss those special times at the end of each day when they read and prayed together in the tiny cabin in the barge. So many things had happened to her through the past few months, and to Will, too. She had to trust that everything would work out in the future, also.

People who worked the canals were very friendly to each other, calling out the latest news as they passed one another or moored alongside each other at night. The only time they were not so friendly was when they were trying to get into a lock or through a tunnel before someone else, for time was money and if they were able to complete their schedule before time, they could earn a bonus and if they were behind time then they were penalised. En route there were places where they had to check in and here they were also able to collect mail. Winnie was very excited when they called into one such station and she received two letters. One was from her Grandfather, telling her that he went every day to look and see if she was coming home.

"It should only be about a week now," Mabel had told her, "I'm pleased for you, for this is no life for a young lady, but I have to be honest. We will miss you so much!"

Winnie's other letter was from Will. She tore open the envelope and inside was a letter written in their special code. Of course, there was no real need to write in code, but she was pleased because it kept their special bond strong. It made her feel good that he hadn't forgotten their language even with all his new friends at school.

This is what he wrote.

"So hwvl Exttxw,

— Dye vlw oyz? X dyjw oyz exrr myyt cwn fvgq ny Clvthbvndwl. X ryaw mgdyyr. So blxwth vth X dvh ney fxc vhawtnzlwm. X exrr nwrr oyz vrr vfyzn ndws xt ndw dyrxhvom.

Ryaw,

Exrr.

You can read the letter working out the code they used. For example, A would be V and V would be A.

e=w=e	b=f=b	k=q=k
i=x=i	g=c=g	l=r=l
o=y=o	d=h=d	m=s=m
u=z=u	j=p=j	n=t=n

Mabel and Dan laughed so much at the strange letter, but since neither of them had been to school or learnt to read and write very much, they would have struggled to have worked it out anyway.

The week soon passed and on the morning when they approached the stile near the Garrow Tunnel where Winnie had first met her Grandfather, she found her stomach turning over with excitement but also nervousness. Mabel had heated water so she could wash all over, then she dressed in her new clothes. Mabel had washed her hair and when it was dry had brushed it until it shone.

They tied up the barge by the side of the canal and loosed Clodhopper to graze on the towpath. Mabel had the kettle on and had managed to bake some scones on the small fire in the living area. Everything was ready and they were all waiting for two o'clock when Grandfather took his walk!

Chapter Eight

Lord Mountjoy-Evans called his dog to heel and told his butler Mason, that he was going for his usual walk down to the canal. It was now October and the days were getting cooler. As he entered the field, in spite of his age, he almost ran through it in excitement because he could see that a narrow boat had moored up. As soon as he reached the stile he saw the smiling face of his granddaughter Winnie, looking very much a young lady – so different from when he had seen her last time!

She ran toward him and gave him a hug and then remembered she was supposed to be a young lady and behave with decorum. So Winnie held out her hand and Lord Mountjoy-Evans shook it solemnly.

"How are you my dear Winifred?" he asked her, "And how are your two kind friends, Dan and Mabel?"

"I am very well, thank you Grandfather," she replied. "Dan and Mabel are, too, but I think they are feeling sad because I am leaving them. Please come down to the boat, because Mabel has baked some scones and put the kettle on to make tea. My belongings are all parcelled up ready to leave.

I'm excited, but a bit sad, too, because they have been so kind to me."

"Of course you are feeling sad, I expected that dear and I have an idea to put to them. Let's go down and have that cup of tea and the thought of a home-made scone is wonderful!"

Dan and Mabel made Grandfather very much at home and he soon talked about his good idea. At least, he thought it was a good one!

"Dan and Mabel," he said, "First of all, I want to say thank you so much for everything you have done for Winnie. My mind has been at ease because I know that you have cared for her as you would your own child. I must admit, I have been walking down to the canal every single day for weeks now, longing for her return! I know, too, that it is hard for you to say goodbye and also to manage without her help. When we talked last you were telling me that you thought maybe you should retire and come to live on the land.

I have been thinking about that and wonder if I can help you. I know the barge belongs to the canal company – but I have a small cottage at the gates to my estate. My gatekeeper has gone into an almshouse and I just wondered if you would like to live in it. There would be light duties, such as opening the gates when carriages come in and out, but it is rent free. The cottage has a large garden where you can grow food and keep chickens and goats. Clodhopper can be stabled with my horses and graze in the meadow and of course, you can see Winnie very often.

I don't expect an instant answer, but if you would like to think it over and let me know, then we can make arrangements."

Winnie was whooping around in delight, in a very unladylike way, but she was so happy to think that Dan and Mabel might live close by.

"Oh Grandfather, what a marvellous idea!" she said, almost knocking over his cup of tea as she tried to hug him. "Oh you will say, 'yes', won't you, Dan and Mabel?" she begged.

They laughed at her and grinned at each other.

"Give us the night to think about it and talk together and ask God if this is his plan for us, love," Dan answered, then turned to Lord Mountjoy-Evans.

"It's a very generous offer, sir. Can we moor here overnight and tell you our answer in the morning? We have been troubled I must say, at the thought of our future. We have to complete our journey to Leeds, but had been wondering if we should now give up hauling coal for the canal company."

A few minutes later Winnie started up the slight hill through the field with her Grandfather, her bundle of clothes under her arm. She had promised to come back in the morning to see Dan and Mabel and Grandfather promised he would come with her and hear their decision.

When Mountjoy Hall came into view it almost took her breath away! It was huge and stately. Was this really to be her home? She tried to think of her dear Mam living in that house. Winnie was sure she would keep getting lost in the large house and grounds. Grandfather squeezed her hand as if to reassure her.

"You'll grow to love it here. Don't worry, I live very simply these days. Wilfred soon found his way around and he tells me that you are five minutes older than he is, so you should do even better!"

Winnie loved the way Grandfather's eyes twinkled when he teased her and she laughed with him.

"I'll do my very best, sir," she said, "But it is very different from my old home and also the barge."

When they reached the house, Mason the butler was introduced. He called Winnie, "Miss Winifred" and she found that quite funny. She felt as if she wanted to look round and see if he was talking to someone else! Mason kept clicking his tongue and saying, "You look just like Miss Ernestina!"

Violet the house maid was then called. She was young and looked very jolly. She took Winnie upstairs to her bedroom.

"I've been lighting the fire every day Miss Winifred, to keep it aired nicely for you. If you go through this door," she told her, opening a small door off the bedroom, "You will see you have your own little room where you can wash and your Grandfather has had one of the new water closets installed for you. He's been so excited ever since he found you and Master Wilfred. He wanted everything to be new in your rooms. I'm sure you'll love it all."

"I'm amazed, Violet," Winnie answered, "I'm awe struck. You should have seen where we used to live and then on the barge we were all squashed up, but it was cosy and fun. Please Violet, could you call me Winnie, I'm not used to being called Winifred all the time."

"Lord Mountjoy-Evans told me this used to be your Mama's room when she was a girl – she had the same bed and wardrobe, but all the bed linen is new. I hope you like it, I helped choose it. I thought you would like the little roses on the bedspread."

"I love it – you chose just perfectly for me," said Winnie, with a smile. "Please Violet, will you be my friend? I do want to make friends here."

"Of course, Miss Winnie, but I am still a servant and you are the Lord's Grandaughter." She said with a smile.

Winnie let Violet hang up her clothes. She had never before owned so many, but they looked so few when they were hung in the large wardrobe. She carefully undid her treasures, too. They were the precious things her mother had given her before she died.

That night she had dinner with her Grandfather in his study. He said the dining room was far too large for only two people, so they used a small table by the fire. Winnie was glad. After dinner she felt very tired and almost fell asleep by the fire. She was used to going to bed very early and getting up early when working on the barge.

Violet helped her to bed – and when she asked Winnie for her nightgown she found that she didn't own such a thing, so Violet opened a drawer and took out a silk nightgown.

"It will be big, but it belonged to your Mama," she told her. It was huge, but Winnie felt so special all wrapped up in the soft silk and knowing that once upon a time her Ma had worn it.

When Violet had said goodnight and left her to sleep, Winnie did feel very alone in the huge room. She missed reading the Bible to Dan and Mabel, but took her little Bible and read her favourite psalm about the Lord being her shepherd and looking after her. Then she put out the gas light and began to talk to Jesus and thank him for all the blessings he had given her. She prayed for her father in Australia, her Grandfather and Will. Then she prayed for Dan and Mabel. "Please, please let them say yes to Grandfather's good idea," she added just before she fell asleep.

The next day Winnie woke very early and at first couldn't think where she was. Then she remembered. She ran to the window and tried to pull back the thick curtains to see if it was a nice day. The sun was shining, but she felt a bit cold, so snuggled under the eiderdown on her lovely bed. She wondered what would happen. Should she get up and washed?

On the bookshelf there were several books. Winnie found one that looked interesting and took it back to bed to read it. Before long, there was a knock at the door and Violet came in with breakfast on a tray. Winnie had never eaten breakfast in bed before. She had a feeling that her life was going to be full of new experiences! While she ate, Violet explained that she would make up the fire in her room and then bring hot water and help her wash and dress.

"But I'm ten years old – and almost eleven!" said Winnie, "I've looked after myself for years!"

"Sure, Winnie, so have I," Violet told her, "But part of my job is to spoil you and help you now that you are a lady!"

Winnie wasn't sure if she really wanted that, but decided that she wouldn't argue – at least not on her first day. Violet was so jolly and it was nice to have someone to talk with.

When she was dressed and ready she was taken down to see her Grandfather who was in his study.

"I'll show you round the rooms which we use – some of them we keep closed up unless we have visitors," he explained. "You can go in all of them, explore and have fun – but I mostly live in the study and library these days. When I've shown you round we'll go down and see how Dan and Mabel are doing, shall we?"

"Oh yes please," Winnie answered, "I do hope they like your idea!"

It was fun exploring the huge old house with Grandfather. There were a lot of large paintings on the walls of some of the rooms and he told her they were her ancestors. The only one I'll tell you about today is this one," he said and he pointed to a lovely picture of a young girl. "It's Mam!" cried Winnie in delight!

When they reached the canal Dan and Mabel were waiting for them.

"Come in my dears," invited Mabel, as they stepped carefully over the plank. Once they were settled and Mabel had brewed some tea, Dan began to speak.

"I know you have come for our answer," he said, clearing his throat, "And Mabel and I are just overcome by your kind offer and we want to accept it. Thank you so much, not just for giving us a home but most of all so that we can still be near Winnie. She is like a grandaughter to us! We know that our own children have nowhere for us to stay even if we asked to be with them. We also know that it is time to give up working the canal. We will miss it though, after all these years. At least we can keep dear old Clodhopper and walk down and see the boats as they pass. No doubt we'll get the news and meet some of our friends that way, too. Thank you for your wonderful idea."

Winnie had never heard Dan say so much at one time – he was a man of few words. Mabel was almost in tears and so was Winnie. Grandfather shook everybody's hand and kept saying how pleased he was.

"It'll be after the winter before we can come, I reckon," said Dan.

"Get a letter to me and then I'll arrange for a carriage to collect you from Leeds," Grandfather told them, and this was agreed.

"Most satisfactory," said Grandfather as he and Winnie walked back to the Hall for luncheon.

Chapter Nine

Len Collins had become used to the routine in prison in Perth. It was far better than the sea journey from England to Australia. He had been sea sick for weeks on end and the quarters on board were so cramped. He thought he would smell of sweat and vomit for the rest of his life. However, it had given him time to think and no opportunity to keep drinking alcohol, which had been the cause of his downfall. He had met with God on that ship and asked for forgiveness for all the wrong he had done through his life and especially for mistreating his wife and abandoning his twins, Will and Winnie.

Life had improved for Len since his arrival In Perth. Of course, the prison conditions were grim, but he was out doors most of the day crushing stone and making roads and although the food was simple fare, it was adequate. He had a few mates among the other prisoners. Most of them were not hardened criminals, but men who had fallen on hard times and made stupid mistakes, which they now bitterly regretted. Some of the men, like himself, had been wrongly accused, for although Len had been drunk and picked a fight with the landlord of 'The Cock and Hen', he knew that he had not attempted to murder him and had never carried a knife. He had been tried, found guilty and sentenced to ten long years of hard labour in the colonies.

Among the other prisoners was a man called Ben, who had also been found guilty of a crime which he had not committed. Ben was a man who had gone to school and could read and write, unlike most of the men. He was a natural leader and had become an overseer of the group of prisoners to which Len belonged. Ben was a Christian and in the evenings he read the Bible out loud and explained it to any of the prisoners who wanted to listen. Len found himself drawn to the little group night after night. He had given his wife a hard time for her faith in God, but now he was beginning to understand more about it. One day he had a talk with Ben, telling him about the anger he had inside and the way he hated himself for all his bad behaviour. He longed to be able to change.

"I want to be different and even if I never get to see my dear children again, I want them to be proud of me, not ashamed, as they must be now."

Ben told him how Jesus could take away the hate and anger and give him a new heart of love and so one night, kneeling under the Australian sky, he asked Jesus to forgive him and change his heart and life. Len knew that Jesus had heard and answered that prayer, for he experienced a peace and lightness in his spirit that helped him work willingly and even enjoyed each day.

The prison was mostly run by British soldiers who were stationed in the colonies to keep peace and order. One morning after breakfast as the men were preparing for the march out to where they were working, an officer approached him.

"Collins Leonard, no 7335086281, report at once to the

Commandant." He was commanded.

"Yes sir," replied Len, wondering what was happening.

When he reached the officers' mess and asked where he could find the Commandant, he was directed to an office in a nearby building. A soldier was guarding the door and asked who he was.

"Leonard Collins sir, reporting as requested," he answered. He was shown into an office where a very important Army official was sitting at a desk. The officer was obviously of a high rank and his uniform was impressive.

He looked up as Len hesitantly walked in.

"Collins Leonard?" he asked.

"Yes sir, no 7335086281" Len replied. His prison number was tattooed on his arm, so he would never be able to forget it.

"I have a communication from London about you," he said, almost kindly.

"Your conviction has been revoked. Another person has testified to your innocence in the crime of attempted murder and someone else arrested and convicted of stabbing the man in question. Your conviction is now a lesser one of causing an affray, which carries the sentence of one year hard labour. You have already served six months here and have a clean record. I have decided to put you in the prison kitchen for the remaining six months, where you can learn the trade of a cook. It will give you a trade you can use in your future life. If you do well you will be given a certificate to say you are trained as a cook and you will be released in six months with the option of free passage back to England or be a free man in this brave new country.

Sometimes, a man needs time to think about making a new start in life. Next March I will call for you again to hear your decision as a ship will sail in early April. Do not abuse the trust we are placing in you. There are temptations in a place like the kitchens. Anyone who steals is punished severely and you could end up crushing rocks for the rest of your life. Do you understand me?"

"Yes sir," answered Len, still trying to take in the good news. Only the week before Ben had been telling the men that God had a future for them.

"You are dismissed. Report to your overseer at once. An officer will collect you in precisely one hour and escort you to the kitchen where you will start work," said the Commandant.

Len almost ran back to his quarters where Ben was checking the men who were about to start the walk to the stone quarry. He shared his news and Ben smiled.

"Good on you!" he said, "Keep praying and God will help you to be a great cook!"

The next few weeks were not at all easy for Len. Most of the time he seemed to be preparing vegetables for a very grumpy head cook – but he kept praying and doing the best he could, all the while watching the cooks as they made dishes. He wanted to learn all he could.

There was something else he wanted to do as well. He wanted to write to the twins and tell them where he was and what had happened to him. He had been trying to learn to read and write, but it was slow work. He now had to work late in the evening several days a week helping to prepare meals for the soldiers, so he wasn't often able to get to Ben's classes. One Sunday they did get an hour together and Len asked his friend if he would do him a favour and write a letter to his children.

It wasn't easy to write to Winnie and Will and beg their forgiveness, tell them about the change in my life, how the sentence has been reduced and why. Len also really wasn't sure about the future. He kept asking God to guide him and show him if he should stay in Australia or return to England.

He longed to know what was happening to his children. Were they managing on their own? Most of all he wanted them to know that he loved them very much and that God loved them, too.

Now that Len was working in the kitchen he had a very small wage each week, enough to buy a piece of soap to wash himself and his clothes and he had saved enough for writing paper, a pencil and a stamp.

Once the letter was written, Len could now sign his own name and the letter was sealed and put into the mail bag. He knew it would take weeks for the mail ship to reach England and then weeks again before he received a reply. He just prayed that he would have a reply before the end of March when he had to make his big decision. It had been a problem knowing where to send the letter. Len's first thought was the workhouse, but then he wondered if it would be given to Will. As he was thinking about this a thought came to him to send it to the minister at St. Cuthbert's church in his home town. So, Ben had written a covering letter to the minister asking him to try and locate the children and get the letter to them.

Knowing the letter was on its way was a great relief to Len. He even sang as he worked away in the kitchen. One day the grumpy head cook called him over.

"You have done well with the vegetables. Now you can start learning to cook them!" he said.

"Thank you cook," said Len, happily. When his wife had been alive he had never dreamed of helping with cooking. In Victorian times, that was definitely the woman's work, even if like his wife, she had been working twelve hours in the mill! Now he was keen to learn and really enjoyed his work. It was the first real job he had ever had!

Len worked very hard for long hours every day but he didn't mind. Often he talked to God in his mind as he worked, always praying for the twins that God would take care of them and they too would have a hope and a future.

Chapter Ten

Early in October a letter was delivered to the house in Addiscombe Road where Mrs Belinda Mountjoy-Evans and her family lived. It had been sent from London and was in a very smart cream envelope. Brownie the footman put the letter on a silver tray along with the silver paper knife used to open letters and carried it to the library where his mistress was sitting drinking tea and reading the morning paper.

He knocked gently on the door before he walked in to hand her the letter. Her eyes lit up – news of her husband at last! It had been over two months since they last had news of the expedition and although that wasn't totally unusual, she just longed to have the reassurance that everything was going well. She knew that the children were all hoping that maybe Papa would get home for Christmas!

Belinda opened the letter carefully and put the knife and the envelope onto the tray – and said 'thank you' to Brownie, who left the room. She always liked the pleasure of reading and then re-reading her husband's letters in private, before sharing any news with the family or the staff.

"My dear Mrs Mountjoy-Evans," it began and with disappointment she realised that it was from the scientific society who had commissioned

the expedition.

"We are very sorry to inform you that we have good reason to believe that your husband, Ernest Mountjoy-Evans, along with his companions, has died. We wished to inform you before we told the public through the press.

Two months ago your husband and colleagues began a trek into the Ituri Forest and Virunga Volcanoes in the Congo. On the way they were waylaid by a group of pygmy men, armed with their poisoned arrows and darts and some of the party were killed instantly. The local Congolese who were carrying the supplies fled into the forest and it took them several weeks to find their way to civilisation to tell the story. The story of the carriers is garbled, it seems some of the men were killed instantly and a few taken captive, but since after weeks of searching the area, there has been no trace of them, it must be presumed they have all died.

Please accept our sincere condolences. We will be sending a money order to cover what would have been your husband's salary until the end of the year.

Yours very sincerely etc.etc."

Mrs Mountjoy-Evans read and reread the letter through the blur of tears in her eyes. She just couldn't take it in. She had always known, of course, that her husband was in a very high risk sort of job, but somehow she had never really thought that he wouldn't come home.

After a few minutes, she began to sob as the news sunk in. She felt very alone in her grief, but knew that she would have to be very strong for the children and also her father in law, who having learnt only a few months ago that his daughter was dead would now have to face the terrible news that his son was dead, too.

After a little while she calmed herself and dried her tears. She had to be brave and strong. From now on she would be the head of the house, but how they would manage without her husband's salary she just did not know.

She walked to the fireplace and rang the bell which was used to call the servants. Brownie came within minutes.

"You called, Madam?" he said, but one look at the face of his mistress told him it was very bad news.

"Please ask Miss Austerberry to bring Libby-Ann, and Polly to bring Elspeth to me. I have very bad news to share with them. Then please tell Cook and Constance that I will want to see you all in the kitchen in an hour's time."

The two children were very surprised to have their lessons interrupted by a visit to their Mama in the morning. The nursery maid and governess brought the girls into the study and were told gently by Mrs Mountjoy-Evans to wait outside until she needed them again.

"Come and sit with me," she said to the girls. "I have something very important to tell you." Elspeth climbed on her Mama's knee and Libby-Ann sat on a little stool nearby.

"I have just received a letter with very, very sad news. Your dear Papa has been attacked by pygmies in the forest and it seems that he and all the other men on the expedition have been killed."

Elspeth was too young to really understand but Libby-Ann was devastated.

"It can't be true!" she said, bursting into tears, "Papa can't be dead. He must come home to us. There is so much I want to show him and tell him!"

"I know darling, but sometimes terrible things happen even to wonderful men like Papa. It's going to be very hard for all of us, but we need to be strong and brave and help each other. I have to try and write to Ernest at school and tell him. It will be terrible for him to get a letter. Maybe, I should go to the school and tell him myself. I just don't know what to do, but we will help each other."

The nursery maid and governess were called in and told the sad news.

"Please take the girls out for a walk and help to comfort them, while I go and tell the rest of the staff," asked Mama.

Everyone in the household was very shocked and it was just so hard for the news to sink in.

Mama wrote at once to Lord Mountjoy-Evans and also to her own parents. She then wrote a letter to Ernest at school, copying the actual words from the letter which she had received. She also wrote a letter to the headmaster. She sent both letters to the head and asked him to break the news gently to her son.

"Sadly, there can be no funeral for him to come home and say 'goodbye'. I wish him to know before it gets into the papers and please protect him if any local reporters try to come and find him," she wrote.

Winnie had been having a riding lesson on the pony which

Grandfather had bought for her. She had called the pony, 'Star' because the white marking on his forehead was a bit like a star. She was so happy now that she was getting used to living in the large house and loved her Grandfather very much. He had promised that very soon she would have lessons at home with a governess and possibly in a year or so go to a day school in the nearest town.

"I am a modern man, for all my age," he had explained, "I think girls should be educated as well as boys. You are a bright girl and will learn well. My dear wife, your grandmother who passed away many years ago, when your mother was just a girl like you, was very clever and always wished she had gone to school. Tina, your Mama, was a very good scholar, too."

Winnie had taken to riding very well and the groom said she was a 'natural'. He helped her down from the pony and she ran into the house with pink cheeks and a big smile. Her Grandfather was sitting in his leather armchair with his dog at his feet and tears were streaming down his eyes.

"Grandfather," she said, "Dear Grandfather, whatever is the matter? What has happened?"

He drew her close and hugged her. "Oh my dear little Winnie, my son Ernest, your uncle, has been killed in the Congo forest. Both my own children are dead. How can I bear it?"

Winnie just didn't know what to say. She just held her Grandfather and kept hugging him until at last he became quiet.

"Thank you dear," he said, "At least I have found you and Will and have Belinda, my daughter in law and her children. We will be brave and help each other."

Many miles away at Wheelie Hall, Ernest wondered why he had been called to the head's office. Had he broken a rule? Were his grades not as good as they should be? He didn't think so, for he did try to work hard and although he had lots of fun he was not wilfully naughty.

He knocked the door timidly and entered. The head held a letter in his hand. Instantly, Ernest's heart plummeted into his shoes.

"Something has happened to Papa?" he asked.

"I'm afraid so, lad. Here is a letter to you from your Mama. Please sit down and read it."

It was all Ernest could do from breaking down and sobbing in front of the headmaster – but he knew he had to hold in his emotions because from a small child he had been taught that boys should not cry.

"Is there someone you would like to talk to?" asked the head, kindly.

Ernest thought a moment and then asked if he could see Joshua, the prefect for whom he fagged.

The head was a little surprised, but rang a bell and sent someone scurrying to find the prefect. Joshua took him to his study and listened to the poor lad read the letter about his father. Tears were in his eyes and the understanding prefect told him to cry. "I will never tell anyone that you cried, but I know my parents would both say it's the best thing you could do when you have to face sad things. Tears were given to us by God to help heal our broken hearts," he told him.

It was a relief to cry – to let out a tiny bit of the pain he was feeling inside. Joshua made him a drink of chocolate – the ultimate luxury at that time and toasted crumpets on the coal fire.

When they had finished eating, Joshua asked if he could pray with Ernest, who nodded. The prayer was for strength and courage to face the future and it helped him to calm down.

Just before Ernest went back to his own class, Joshua read the letter and the copy of the letter which his mother had received.

"You know, Ernest, there might be just a slim chance that your father is alive. It says that the men are presumed dead as nothing has been heard from them and no bodies found. I don't want to give you false hope, but I feel somehow that the Lord wants me to tell you that. Maybe to pray that if they are dead someone will find the bodies, but if they are alive, then they will be found."

"Thank you, Joshua, thank you. It will help having something positive to pray for. Pray for me that I will be brave enough to tell my friends about this news and to carry on as Papa would want me to. I will have to be the man of the house now. Mama will need my support."

On his way back to the Upper Third Ernest remembered how he had found the ambergris in the summer holidays, which was worth so much money. The money had been kept safely in the bank. It comforted him to know that he had some money which would help his mother.

Chapter Eleven

The weeks had gone by and the three men who had been taken captive by the pygmies in the Ituri Forest were becoming used to their strange routine. Yes, they were prisoners, but they had quite a lot of freedom. They had tried many times to think of plans to escape, but they all seemed too risky since they were at all times guarded by a few young men who carried poisoned arrows and were known never to miss their aim.

Ernest Mountjoy-Evans was a butterfly collector and had been on several expeditions before in different parts of the world. He had experienced some quite hair-raising adventures before, but nothing quite as scary as this one. He was glad he was not alone, but had Richard, a botanist and David an entomologist with him. They had been sharing a tent when the raid had happened and had not only escaped with their lives, but had also, amazingly, managed to save some of their notes and specimens.

Even after these weeks of captivity they really had no idea why they had been captured. It seems it might have been a mistake and the Pygmies had thought they were enemies. They had become accustomed to eating strange creatures and roots and berries, but had kept well, although they were all getting very thin. They had tried to learn some of the language spoken by their captors, and to make friends with them. In fact it seemed that that pygmy women and children were now so used to their strange white skin that they no longer ran away and hid from them. They had needed to do something to keep fit and help the time go by, so helped the women to dig a garden and plant crops.

The group of pygmies seemed reluctant to move from the village where they were holding the men captive – although normally, they were always moving to fresh areas to hunt. It was such a strange situation and the three men wondered how long it would continue. All their Congolese helpers had fled when the raid had taken place and their other colleagues had been murdered. They thought that perhaps by now news would have reached the outside world and a search party sent out to look for them.

David had a Bible and even before the capture he had been discussing his Christian faith with his two tent mates and they had come to believe in Jesus as their Saviour, too. These weeks together had given them time to learn so much from the Bible and trust God in very practical ways to help them every day. They had been praying every night for their families and asking the Lord to be merciful and allow them to one day see them again. Some days were good and it was easier to trust, other days they were depressed and thought they might never get out of the forest. The weather had recently changed, too. Instead of dry and reasonably warm weather, the rains had started and it was cold. Up in the mountains it can be very cold and the rain was heavy. It seeped through the grass roof on the tiny mud hut which was their prison. Even their pygmy guards seemed cold and miserable.

The day dawned about six am and the pygmy camp stirred. The young men who had guarded them through the night went to rest as others took over. Everything seemed the same as usual as the women began to fry ants and grubs on a hot stone in the fireplace. The men were glad to crouch near to the small fire to warm themselves.

"Let's thank God for this food," said Richard, "Even though I really would love eggs and bacon and a hot cup of tea!"

"Don't talk about it!" said Ernest, "I can't even bear to think of such wonderful food. It's hard to be grateful for this, but it's better than nothing!"

As they were eating, suddenly they heard wild, excited cries. Everyone in the village was on their feet, grabbing things and running away! The men got up, wondering whatever was happening. They were definitely forgotten as everyone ran into the forest.

The men looked around, fearful as to what might happen to them. Then they saw the reason for the confusion. There were gorillas in the garden! A whole family of them − a huge male silverback, several females, some with babies and a group of younger animals, not babies but not yet mature.

The men stared in wonder at the beasts. The pygmies were obviously terrified and had all disappeared.

"Maybe this is our God given opportunity to escape," said David. "Let's not make a noise to startle the gorillas, but quietly collect our few belongings and try to head out of here."

It took about five minutes for them to collect their thoughts and their possessions and put on their backpacks. The pygmies had fled deep into the forest, so the men decided to try and trek in the opposite direction. They found a narrow path and headed out, moving as quietly as they could. It was raining and the path was slippery, but they prayed quietly that God would lead them to safety. The forest was a very dangerous place – full of wildlife, like snakes which could harm them and they were grateful for David's knowledge of insects, as even they could be lethal. The men hardly dared to speak, they were so afraid of being recaptured. Every now and then they were startled by a noise echoing through the forest as the silverback beat on his chest and roared, declaring to all that the garden was his territory now. No wonder the pygmies were scared. He was far larger than the largest man among them! The men knew that the pygmies were marvellous trackers and could soon find them, but were so scared of the gorillas they would be unlikely to follow them until the gorillas left the garden and territory around the village.

"Lord, keep those gorillas in our garden," prayed Ernest. "Please give us a few hours to get away and show us which paths to take."

The men continued on the path, listening for every twig which crackled – their nerves taut and their hair almost standing on end with fear. In spite of their meagre breakfast they were beginning to feel hungry again and also very thirsty. They found some of the broad leaves on the plants had drops of water and they licked these to get moisture. After a couple of hours they began to relax a little and stopped briefly to thank God together for their getaway. They asked for guidance and help. They had no idea where they were and the forest covered a huge, almost totally unpopulated area.

They walked another hour or so and were beginning to feel very weary and faint, for they were all undernourished and thin and weak from lack of exercise. Then, ahead of them they saw a clearing and heard the noise of a mountain stream. As they reached the clearing they realised that they had discovered their old camp from which they had been taken as prisoners!

"How amazing!" said Richard. "There are still a few things here! We can salvage things to help us on our journey – look, there's a bit of tent canvas which would make a covering for us at night!"

The men collected what they could, still very cautiously and quietly. They made a pile and then decided how much they could each carry and what they needed most. It was hard to leave some things behind, but they had to be selective and take the things needed most for their survival. "Oh, thank God!" David said with great feeling, "I've found a penknife!"

"Fantastic!" said Ernest, "I hope it's still sharp because there are a couple of tins of food on the ground near by where the old cook house of the camp had been. I left them there as it was no good if we couldn't open them."

The men were ravenous and the thought of some tinned meat was so inviting that they attacked the tins with the penknife and one way or another managed to open them and have the best meal they had eaten in weeks! They kept the tins for using to collect water from the stream. Feeling so much better and very much more cheerful they continued on their way, even though they now had heavier loads to carry.

Through the afternoon they even dared to talk more freely and sing a song or two as they trekked through the forest. The rain eased and the sun came out, warming them and drying their clothes. The sun had also brought out an amazing butterfly which Ernest had never seen before! It was just the sort of creature he had come to the Congo to find. He pointed it out to his friends and they agreed to rest and allow Ernest to try to catch it. He followed the butterfly as it flew up stream. Its wings dazzled as they reflected in the crystal clear water. Then still following it he came to a waterfall. It almost seemed as if the butterfly was leading Ernest and it disappeared behind the falling water. Ernest followed and discovered a cave behind the waterfall which was dry and would be a great place for the three men to stay for the night.

Quickly retracing his steps he called to Richard and David to follow him and he took them to the waterfall. The butterfly was still dancing around. To Ernest it seemed almost like an angel sent by God to protect them. The men were able to set up a camp in the cave and collect twigs and even get a small fire lit, in the way the pygmy women did. They boiled water in one of the empty tins and hunted round for some of the fruits and roots which they now knew were safe to eat. Richard walked down the stream away from the waterfall and tried to fish – but decided he would need more practice and would have to try to make a line with a hook or make a spear if he was to ever catch any.

It felt so good to be free! The men thanked God for the gorillas in the garden and for showing them the cave. With some blankets they had found at the old camp site, they settled for the night, thanking God for their blessings, even though they knew they might not make it to safety for a long time, they felt that God had delivered them and was protecting and leading them.

Chapter Twelve

October had been a sad month for the Mountjoy-Evans family as they came to terms with the letter which had told them all about the terrible way in which the expedition to the Congo had ended. At school, Ernest had sought out his cousin Will and told him about the letter, indeed, allowed him to read exactly what his mother had written. It brought the two boys closer together, for Will had known what it meant to have his mother die and his father be taken far away. He also had grown to love his Grandfather in the short time he had lived with him before starting school at Wheelie Hall.

Now that the woods were being excavated and the boys could no longer use the old ruins as a den, they had taken to meeting up on Saturday mornings in the cricket pavilion because it wasn't used during the winter term and although the inside was locked up, they were able to use the veranda which went around the entire building. Sometimes, they talked about the exciting adventures they'd had through the term, especially the news about the monastery and the artefacts which were being found in the pond. Some wonderful treasures had been recovered and soon would be on display in the local museum. Their history teacher had promised them an outing to view them.

They always ended their time praying for each other's family – with Ginger's parents in Uganda, Will's father in Australia and Ernest still holding on to the little tiny hope that his father could still be alive in the Congo, there was plenty to pray for. Although everything in their tuck boxes had been eaten long ago, the tuck shop at the school opened on Saturdays and the boys shared their pocket money and bought a few sweets. If it was a cold day they just had fun running around and kicking a ball to keep themselves warm. The three boys were now firm friends and sometimes Ernest's friend, Sam joined them, too, which made the numbers even when they played games.

As November drew near the boys were allowed to help sweep up the leaves fallen from the trees in the grounds and collect twigs, because one tradition in the school was to have a November 5th Guy Fawkes celebration with a bonfire. The school cooks made toffee apples and everyone from both sections of the school celebrated around the bonfire. It brightened up the rather dull month and the boys could really have some fun.

December was always a busy month as the school choirs began to prepare for the carol service at the end of term. Many parents came to the service and then took their boys home afterwards for the Christmas holiday. This year Will and Ernest's Grandfather had decided that both families should celebrate Christmas at his house.

After he'd had the sad news from his daughter in law he at once wrote to her insisting that the family all come to him for the Christmas and New Year holiday.

"You see, my dear Belinda," he wrote to his son's wife, "After my wife died and my children had grown up I used to wonder why I was left alone. I prayed that God would also take me and sometimes was angry that I was left to live in this huge house all alone. Now I realise that although I cannot ever be a father to my grandchildren, they all need me very much as a Grandfather. I think we need to make this a special time for all the children- they all will miss their fathers, but the twins have no mother either. I also want to talk to you about their futures, for I have more money than I could ever spend so want to invest it in their lives. So, please humour this old man and come to visit me. If your cook and footman and the nursery maid would like to come, too, that would help my very small staff."

Back in Addiscombe, Belinda Mountjoy-Evans didn't really need to think long about Grandfather's proposal. It would do them all good to have a change and Libby-Ann had asked several times when would she be able to meet her cousin Winnie. She knew her faithful household staff would gladly come with her and she could also take Rex and even Rafiki with her.

Letters began to flow between Mountjoy Hall and the house in Addiscombe Road. It was arranged that they would travel by train and be collected from the station at Skipton. Cook had offered to go ahead of the main party, so that she could help prepare for their arrival. They would come before the end of the school term, so that as a great surprise for Ernest, she and Grandfather and possibly Winnie and Libby-Ann would be at the school carol service.

Meanwhile, Miss Austerberry kept Libby-Ann very busy making presents for her family. Even though she hated sewing, she tried hard to make some pin cushions for her Mama and cousin and then she had much more fun making fudge and toffee for Grandfather and the boys. It was nice to do happy things again, even though she had to wear a black dress and armband all the time out of respect for her father, just as her mother did. Somehow, she couldn't quite believe her Papa was really and truly gone forever. It was so hard when there had been no burial and there was no grave to visit.

Winnie too, was excited about meeting her cousin. She missed the hard work of the canal and sometimes became restless, so was delighted when Grandfather asked her to help cut holly, mistletoe and ivy to decorate the house. She helped the servants clean and polish and also Cook with some baking. Mabel had taught her how to make lovely scones and she made biscuits, too.

About ten days before Christmas a visitor came to Mountjoy Hall. Winnie recognised him at once. He was the kind vicar at St. Cuthbert's Church. The last day she had seen him was the day when she had run away to the canal. She knew that he had been kind to Will, rescuing him from the workhouse and getting him his post as a student teacher in Skipton. He had ridden over in his pony and trap and Grandfather was very pleased to see him. Winnie was asked to come into the library and pour out the tea for them and it made her feel very grown up being able to do that.

After a little while of greeting each other and chatting, the vicar told Grandfather and Winnie the real reason for his visit.

"Yesterday a letter was delivered to the vicarage," he said. "It was addressed to me, with a covering letter to explain that your Father,

Winnie, wanted to try to get a letter to you and Will and as he had no idea where you both were living, he sent it to me, thinking I might be able to find you both. He certainly sent it to the right person! It must have been God guiding him".

"But Pa can't read or write," began Winnie, but was quickly interrupted by the Vicar.

"He dictated his letter and it has been written down for you by someone else … anyway, here it is. It is to you and Will, so you can open it."

"Thank you, sir," said Winnie and took the letter. Her Grandfather took a letter opener from his desk and helped her open the envelope. Two sheets of paper full of small, neat writing were inside.

"You can go to your room and read it in private, dear," suggested her Grandfather, "It will give the minister and I time to chat. You can tell us about the letter later if you wish to share its contents. Then I know you will keep it safely for when Will comes home in a week or so."

Winnie needed no second bidding and ran upstairs to her room. As it was winter Violet kept a fire burning in the grate all day, so it was cosy. She climbed into the comfy chair by the fire and unfolded the letter and began to read.

"My dear Winnie and Will," the letter began,

"I am asking my great friend Ben to write this letter for me, for although I am slowly learning to read and write I could not yet manage to write a letter.

First of all, I want to ask you both to forgive me for the way I neglected you and how badly I treated you and your dear mother before she died. I have asked God to forgive me and I know he has, but now, although I don't deserve it, I beg your forgiveness.

As you no doubt learnt, I got into a fight and although I started the fight and the landlord of 'The Cock and Hen' was badly hurt, I was not the one with the knife and I did not stab him. However, I was convicted and deported to Perth, Australia for ten years of hard labour. In some ways, I thank God, because it has brought me to my senses and like the prodigal son in the Bible, I have repented and returned to God my Father."

Then the Twin's father explained all about the sentence being shortened and how he was now training as a cook and how he could possibly return to England during the following year, but did not know what to do. He asked the children to pray for him to make the right decision.

"I long to know what has happened to both of you. If you receive this letter, please can you write back to me and send it to the address on the top of this letter, then Ben will receive it and read it to me. Above all, I pray that you are safe and well and can find it in your hearts to forgive me.

God bless you,

With fondest love,

Pa"

Winnie was quite overcome as she read the letter. She had often thought about her Pa and prayed for him. With Dan and Mabel's help she had forgiven him long ago for his treatment of the family. Now she felt thrilled to know that the Good Shepherd had found her Pa, too and hoped he would come home again. Winnie hoped that Will would feel the same. She would always remember Will's face as he said goodbye to her and went with Pa to the workhouse. It had been terrible for him. Then Winnie also wondered how her Grandfather would feel about the news. She knew that he was so happy to have her and Will as part of the family once again. Would that all change? If Pa came home and they went to live with him would they be very poor again and Will have to leave his new school? There were so many questions in Winnie's mind. She felt all mixed up and needed some space to think, so decided to talk to her pony in the stables. That was the nice thing about animals – you could tell them everything and they listened to you!

As Winnie thought that thought, she remembered that Mabel had told her she could talk to Jesus about anything at any time and he would always listen, too.

Her pony, Star, was pleased to see her and the apple she had asked Violet to give her for him. She spent some time grooming him and talking to him and Jesus at the same time. It helped her to feel much better and by the time she had to go and wash ready for her lunch, she felt quite calm once more.

The Rev. Franklin had enjoyed his chat with Lord Mountjoy-Evans. He was pleased to hear how well Will was doing at school and how Winnie had settled into life at the Hall. The two men were becoming good friends and they both cared deeply for the children. Grandfather asked the minister to join them for lunch. Winnie was able to chat about the letter and give the men the good news about her father.

"I thought perhaps I would wait until Will comes home next week and then we could write a letter back. I need to talk to him and to you as well, dear Grandfather, before I answer it."

"That's very wise, Winnie", said her Grandfather, "and thank you for telling us the news. I think this family is due for some good news. I have had an idea, too. Why don't we get out the carriage and go back to Skipton market and do some Christmas shopping. All the family will be here very soon and we must get ready."

"Oh what a lovely idea," said Winnie, "I'd love to do that."

So after lunch they said goodbye to Rev. Franklin and drove over to Skipton to shop. Grandfather had given Winnie some pocket money to spend and also he had made a list of things he wanted to buy to make this Christmas an extra special time for his family.

Chapter Thirteen

The day after the trip to Skipton, Cook arrived from Addiscombe and was collected at Skipton station. She quickly settled in at the Hall. Winnie liked her at once; she was jolly and kind and let her help with cooking.

Violet allowed Winnie to help her air the spare rooms, make up the beds and get everything ready for the visitors. The dining room was dusted and the silver cutlery polished. The whole house had an air of busyness and began to look very Christmassy. The groom had cut a huge log, a Yule log, Grandfather called it, which was put in the drawing room. He told Winnie that it would keep burning all the way from Christmas until New Year! There were wonderful smells coming from the kitchen as the two cooks prepared some of the food! A couple of extra girls had been hired from the village, who would help as kitchen maids while the visitors were staying.

The day when Aunt Belinda was due to arrive with her two cousins Libby-Ann and Elspeth, Winnie was almost beside herself with excitement. Grandfather promised to take her with him to Skipton to meet the train. The groom was to drive the other carriage, for with Brownie and Polly coming with the family, plus a dog and a parrot, they would need all the space they could find. The family would be very tired for they were leaving London early in the morning and not arriving until late evening.

Winnie was dressed in her warmest clothes and a thick blanket wrapped around her knees. It was dark as they set off, but it was a clear and moonlit night and she could look at the stars. She still remembered the constellations which Dan had taught her when she was working on the canal. It was lovely to sit beside Grandfather and chat to him. She had endless questions to ask about her cousins, which he patiently tried to answer. Eventually, she fell asleep listening to the 'clip-clop' of the horses' hooves on the road.

At Skipton her Grandfather gently woke her up.

"We're here Winnie and by the whistle of the train, I think the family is here, too. Let's meet them." He lifted Winnie down from the carriage and held her hand. It was as if he knew that she was suddenly feeling shy about meeting everybody. What if they didn't like her? They were 'posh' people and she was only just beginning to learn to be ladylike and wasn't very good at it, either.

The porters were opening the carriage doors and Grandfather went quickly to the first class coach where he began to help a lady, who she guessed was her Aunt Belinda. Libby-Ann was next then Polly who carried a very sleepy little Elspeth followed by Brownie who was getting all their luggage from the guard's van.

Libby-Ann ran up to her and hugged her. "You must be Winnie," she said, "I'm so glad to meet you. It'll be such fun having you as my friend!" Winnie found her shyness melting away and she knew she and Libby-Ann would have a great time together. Libby-Ann was allowed to sit alongside Winnie and Grandfather, while Aunt Belinda, Polly and Elspeth were inside the carriage. Brownie and the luggage and the pets were in the smaller carriage which was driven by the groom. It took a long time to drive back to Mountjoy Hall, but the two girls were chatting away as if they were long lost friends just reunited, much to Grandfather's delight and amusement.

The next day the family from Addiscombe were all very tired and Grandfather made sure they all rested well. He had another surprise lined up for Winnie. It had taken quite a lot of arranging with the Rev. Franklin of St. Cuthbert's. The minister drove over to Mountjoy Hall early in the morning in his pony and trap.

"I'm taking you to see some friends," he announced to Winnie. At once she was excited, but afterwards just a little scared, thinking she may be going near where they used to live and where she thought the landlord of 'The Cock and Hen' still lived. She didn't know that he was safely in prison and couldn't harm her.

"Who are we going to visit?" she asked the minister.

He laughed and spoke in a riddle, "That's for me to know and you to wait and see!" Winnie guessed she would just have to trust him, for he was a good man and Grandfather's friend and indeed, wait and see.

Once again she had a warm blanket over her knees and a basket of goodies which the two cooks had baked. Violet was travelling with her because she was having a day off to visit her Mam and Pa in a village near Skipton.

"Christmas is so exciting, isn't it?" Violet said to Winnie. "This will be the best one since I began work at the Hall because Lord Mountjoy has the family and everywhere is decorated and everyone is happy."

"Well, yes and no," replied Winnie, "For Will and me it is wonderful. We have a home now and a Grandfather and a letter telling us that our Pa is safe and well, but Aunt Belinda and her family have just had such sad news. It must be terrible if someone you love dies a long way from home. You can't have a funeral like we did for Mam."

"Yes, I must remember that," answered Violet, "I have never met Mr Ernest because he has always been abroad when the family have come to stay. I do so hope they have a happy Christmas in spite of their loss."

They stopped to let Violet off the pony and trap and she went running down the garden path with a basket of baking for her parents. She waved to Winnie and they started again towards Barnsoldwick. After the late night meeting her relatives from the train, she began to feel sleepy and dozed off for a while. When she woke again Winnie saw they were in a little town and heading down Coronation Street towards the canal. They stopped at the bottom of the road and Rev. Franklin helped her down. Together they walked under the canal bridge and there moored at the side was 'Bright Water' with Clodhopper tethered to a post on the tow path.

Winnie squealed with delight and walked the gangplank with the basket of baking. It was just like coming home again! There were hugs all round and happy greetings! Dan and Mabel had been visited by the minister and so were ready for the surprise. They were so happy to see Winnie again. She talked non-stop about everything which had happened over the last couple of months and they told her that they were giving up their life on the canal as soon as they reached Leeds. Then they would move to live in the gate house at Mountjoy Hall. They hoped to move in when the spring arrived!

"Our sons will help us do the move," said Dan, "Not that we have many things. We don't need them on a barge and I guess we won't need much in a small cottage. Our children all plan to visit us and see that we and Clodhopper are happy and well."

"That's so wonderful," said Winnie, "It's a like a Christmas present to know you are coming and spring will soon arrive!"

"Talking of presents, ducks," Mabel said, going to her tiny cupboard in the living area of the narrow boat and taking out something wrapped in newspaper. "This is for you with our love. Not to be opened until Christmas!"

"Thank you so much," said Winnie, feeling the shape and trying to guess what might be inside.

"And this basket is for you, too. The cooks have made them, but I have helped as well."

Dan and Mabel were delighted with the goodies and thanked Winnie.

"Now I reckon we all need a good brew," Mabel announced as she took the boiling kettle and began to make tea.

It was a lovely visit and Winnie found it hard to say goodbye when it was time to leave. It helped knowing that her dear friends would soon be living very near.

"We have one more stop to make before we pick up Violet," announced Rev. Franklin. "My sister in Skipton would like us to eat luncheon with her and she wants to send a present to Will. She loved having Will help with her school and enjoyed teaching him in the evenings."

So they drove up the drive of the Georgian house where she lived and rang the bell. The maid answered and took them inside while the groom who had been Will's friend when he had lived and worked there, took the pony to give him some food and drink.

They had a lovely luncheon and Winnie could hear the children in the school during their lunch break. Afterwards they went to the main classroom and the children sang some carols for the visitors. Then some of the small children gave a package to Winnie. The children had been making cards for Will and before they left, Miss Franklin gave Winnie a package wrapped in brown paper asking her to give it to Will at Christmas.

After they had said goodbye to Miss Franklin, they drove on to collect Violet, who was waiting for them, looking out of the parlour window through the thick lace curtain. She and Winnie chatted all the way home about the visits they had made.

"Thank you so much for taking me and giving me such a special day," Winnie said as she was helped down from the trap.

"I've enjoyed taking you my dear," replied the Rev. Franklin.

The next day Winnie and Libby-Ann spent the whole day together. They made some paper chains to hang up in the hall. Then Winnie took her cousin to see her pony Star, in the stables.

"I'm only just learning to ride him and take care of him," she told Libby-Ann, then asked her, "Can you ride?"

"A little, but I don't have my own pony," she answered.

"Then you must share Star whenever you are here," said Winnie, generously. "You can borrow my riding clothes if you like, we are about the same size."

"You are so kind!" exclaimed Libby-Ann, "I'd so love to have a ride. I hate staying in all day, but Mama says it's too cold to go for many walks or just to play outside."

After lunch the two girls went to the stables and the groom was quite happy to let them ride. Winnie found it so much fun to have someone her own age to play with.

That evening the two girls dressed in their best dresses and went to have dinner in the large dining room. Elspeth still had her dinner with Polly in the old nursery rooms at the top of the house.

"My, how grown up you both look!" said Grandfather. "We'll have to watch you tomorrow, the boys will all be making eyes at you!"

The girls started to giggle, then Libby-Ann asked her Grandfather, "But which boys, Grandpapa? Ernest and Will are still at school!"

"Tomorrow is another surprise. Life is full of surprises you know, some not so nice, but most of them are great and can be real adventures!" he said with a smile. "We are all going by train to Wheelie Hall to collect the boys – your Mama, you two girls and myself." Grandfather chuckled to himself. "We'll surprise the boys!"

Chapter Fourteen

The following day Brownie drove Grandfather, Winnie, Libby-Ann and her Mother to the station early in the morning and they caught a train to Leeds. From Leeds it was just a short distance to Wheelie Hall. They arrived towards the end of the morning and went at once to the school chapel, just in time for the carol service.

The chapel was full with parents and students and everyone joined in singing the wonderful Christmas carols and hymns and listened to readings from the Bible. Libby-Ann felt very proud because Ernest had been chosen to do one of the readings. He looked so smart in his school uniform, but also wore a black armband because he was in mourning. It was the custom to do this, just as the girls and women wore black clothes to mourn the loss of someone they loved. Indeed, Queen Victoria's husband, Prince Albert, had been dead for several years, but the queen still wore black clothes.

At the end of the service the parents were invited to take refreshments in the school refectory and then the boys filed out class by class. Will spotted Grandfather and Winnie sitting near the back and went pink with excitement. He had no idea they were coming and neither had Ernest whose class was the next to leave. How wonderful, his Mama had heard him read! He was so pleased to see her and Libby-Ann.

The boys soon found their family and as soon as they had all eaten, they took them around both the prep and the senior school and introduced them to their close friends.

"We must ask for your trunks to be taken to the station," said Grandfather to the boys, "We need to leave soon to catch the train to Skipton."

There was plenty of time on the train for talking and for the cousins to get to know each other. Grandfather and Belinda were happy to see how well they were getting on. The boys told the girls all about the term's adventures.

"We heard only last week something about the skeleton which I found in the well and was thought to be a child called Lucy, who had got lost and was never found. Her present day relatives have been traced and they wish to have a proper burial for her body. They will have it in the new year when we are back at school and have asked that Ginger and I attend the service," Will told everyone. "I'm really pleased because sometimes I still dream about finding the skeleton, but I'm sure the dreams will stop once she is properly buried."

Then they talked about the old monastery ruins which were being excavated and the treasure which had been found in the lake.

"It seems you have had great adventures at school," remarked Grandfather, "But I hope you have been studying as well!"

"We have!" chorused Will and Ernest together.

"In fact, Grandfather," said Ernest, "Will is amazing. He's so good at Latin and Greek he's been helping me. I've been helping him learn French, because it was a new subject for him. I wish we were in the same class and did study hall together!"

Will went a little pink with embarrassment as his cousin praised him, but he knew it was true. His time with Rev. Franklin's sister helping at her school and studying in the evenings had put him top of the class in these two ancient languages.

It had been a long day and they were all glad to get home to Mountjoy Hall. It was only a couple of days until Christmas and there was so much they wanted to do.

One of the first things which Ernest wanted to do was to spend some time alone with his Mama. He needed to talk to her and say he knew it was almost impossible, but he felt inside that Papa might still be alive. There was surely just a tiny hope.

"I know I am wearing the armband, but I still hope and pray maybe Papa is still alive," he told his Mama, "but if Papa did die then I want you to have all the money from the ambergris I found in the summer holidays. You will need the money."

"That is very kind and thoughtful of you," said his Mama, "but it may not come to that. Grandfather has said that he would like us to sell our house and move up here. Just as he has taken the responsibility of providing for your cousins, so he promises to provide for us all. I have decided that I will pray and ask God to show me the way forward, but I am grateful for his kind offer. It's too soon to make many decisions. I have accepted that Papa will not come home, but am not yet ready to move house. For all our sakes, we need to try to be happy and enjoy this Christmas, for that is what Papa would want."

Out in the stables Winnie was showing her pony to Will. Then they sat on a bale of straw and she gave Will the letter she had received the week before from their Pa. He was amazed as he read it.

"I didn't think we would ever hear from him again," he said to Winnie, "But I'm so glad we have. I feel that we should forgive him because that is what Jesus tells us to do in the Lord's Prayer, isn't it?

"Forgive us our trespasses as we forgive those who trespass against us," Will quoted.

"I'm so glad you feel like that, too. I wasn't sure you would, because he sent you to the workhouse. Let's write to him today and ask someone to take it to the post office to get a stamp to send it to Australia."

So while Ernest, Libby-Ann, Elspeth and their Mama went for a walk by the canal that afternoon, the twins asked their Grandfather if they could have paper and an envelope to write to their father. He suggested they use his study because he had an important job to attend to on the estate.

Once the letter was written to their Pa, Brownie said he would drive them to Skipton so that they could post it as Groom was helping Grandfather. In fact, Cook came along too, as she wanted some things from the shops, so they had quite an outing. When they had finished all the shopping and arrived back at Mountjoy Hall, they were amazed to see Grandfather and the groom hauling in a very large fir tree. They planted it in a bucket and set it up in the entrance hall.

"This is a Christmas tree," he told them all, "One of the new ideas which Prince Albert brought to our country. We've never cut one before, but I thought this would be a great time to start having one!"

The children all clapped and suggested things which they could use as decorations. The lovely scent of the fir tree filled the hall.

"We need a star to put on the very top," suggested Libby-Ann. Winnie and I could make one and paint it yellow, couldn't we?" she said, looking at her cousin.

"Yes, that's a great idea," responded Winnie, "And I think we should send the boys out to find fir cones, which we could paint as well and hang on the branches."

The boys took Rex and also Grandfather's dog, Goldie with them and went to fill a basket with cones.

Elspeth wanted to help, too, so Polly took her to the kitchen where the two cooks were making biscuits. She helped to cut them into shapes. Then the cooks poked holes in the top of each one with a meat skewer and baked them on the range.

"When they are cool we will ice them and then put ribbon through the holes so they can hang on the tree, too." She was told.

That evening they were able to decorate the tree with everything they had been making. It did look splendid. Then Grandfather put out the gas light and lit some candles. They sat around the tree and sang carols and he told them the story of how Jesus was born in Bethlehem.

Just before they went to bed, parcels began to arrive from all over the house where they had been hidden and were placed under the tree.

"This Christmas tree is the most wonderful idea, Grandfather," said Winnie, "Thank you for thinking of it."

"Somehow, this is a very special Christmas," said Libby-Ann. "I know I wanted Papa to be home, but I am learning that God knows best and doesn't make mistakes. I'm so glad we are here with you, Grandfather and I know my cousins!"

The whole of the Christmas time was lovely. Everyone had worked so hard to make gifts and cards for each other. They played lots of games together which Grandfather had bought for them. The Yule log burned brightly and kept them warm, even when it began to snow. In fact, it snowed off and on for several days. There was enough snow for the children to go outside and play snowballs, build a snowman and use the old sledge which Grandfather had unearthed from a corner of the coach house. They had so much fun! Although there were lots of tumbles and falls, no-one was hurt. The dogs loved the snow, too. They were just as excited as the children. Indoors, Rafiki, the parrot, talked to everybody who came into the parlour, which was where his cage had been put. Mostly, he spoke in English, telling everyone to "be quiet and be good!" but every now and then he would lapse into a language he must have learnt many, many years ago in Africa.

"Jambo, jambo sana," he would say, followed by, "Habari gani? Musuri sana!" and "kwa heri, genda musuri," The children thought it very funny and laughed at him. Ernest and Will decided to try and teach him Latin, but didn't have much success.

The days seemed to pass so quickly and soon it was New Year's Eve. Mama and Grandfather had decided that although Elspeth needed to go to bed, everyone else could stay up and hear the bells which would ring out from the village church to mark the passing of 1866 and the start of 1867.

After dinner they played 'Sardines', grownups and children together. It was huge fun finding places to hide, although at times it was a bit scary as the house was so large that it could take ages to find where the person had hidden. The cellar and the bedrooms which were being used were 'out of bounds', but there were so many other rooms to explore and places to hide. The only problem was that the dogs joined in and kept barking, giving away the hiding places!

Just before midnight Grandfather gathered everyone together around the Christmas tree.

"Before we welcome in the New Year," he said, "I want to say thank you to God for many things in the past year. Although we have had some really sad times, God has given me back Tina's children and brought Ernest Senior's family to me this Christmas and I am so grateful to have you all. Most of all, God has forgiven me for my hard and bitter heart and has accepted me into His family. We don't know what next year will hold, but we do know who holds the future. God bless my dear family!"

They all drank a toast in the mulled wine which Cook had made and then crossed their arms and sang, 'Auld Lang Syne' together. A whole new year lay ahead.

Far away, three men were scrambling down the mountains, tired and weary. The daytime temperature had become hotter as the rainy season ended and the dry season began. The men were so exhausted and thin they almost looked like skeletons and their clothes were torn, their hair matted and they had grown long beards.

"Look!" said David, "There are huts! We've made it to a village!"

"Thank God," said Ernest, in a heartfelt way. "Have you got enough energy to walk by moonlight?

We could reach civilisation by dawn!"

"Let's try," said Richard, "It's New Year's Eve, if my calculations are right. A new year we never thought we'd live to see! Thank God for the gorillas in the garden!"

Early in the morning, the three men stumbled into a small town. They were safe at last!